SAP Certified Application Associate

CRM Fundamentals with SAP CRM 7.0 EhP1

By

C Rawat & B Cole

Copyright Notice

Table of Contents

Before you Start..

Before you start here are some Key features of the SAP CRM Associate Certification Exam.

- ✓ The **SAP Certified Application Associate - CRM Fundamentals with SAP CRM 7.0 EhP1** certification test verifies proven skills and fundamental knowledge in the area of the SAP Customer Relationship Management.
- ✓ It proves that the candidate has a good overall understanding within this consultant profile and can implement this knowledge practically in projects under guidance of an experienced consultant.
- ✓ The exam is Computer based and you have three Hours to answer 80 Questions.
- ✓ The Questions are (mostly) multiple choice type and there is NO penalty for an incorrect answer.
- ✓ Some of the Questions have more than one correct answer. You must get ALL the options correct for you to be awarded points.
- ✓ For questions with a single answer, the answers will have a button next to them. You will be able to select only one button.
- ✓ For questions with multiple answers, the answers will have a 'tick box' next to them. This allows you to select multiple answers.
- ✓ You are not allowed to use any reference materials during the certification test (no access to online documentation or to any SAP system).
- ✓ The Official Pass percentage is 65%. (This can vary slightly for your exam)
- ✓ In this book, unless otherwise stated, there is only one correct answer.

A Quick Quiz

Q1. You have replicated the Organization Structure from ECC to CRM. During Business partner replication from CRM to ECC, there is an issue and the replication is not successful. Initial analysis indicates a problem with "Sales Area" missing.

What would you do to investigate the problem? (More than one option is correct)

a) Check if distribution channel & division are assigned to your Sales Org in PPOMA_CRM
b) Check erroneous BDOC messages in ECC.
c) Check RFC connections
d) Create buffer for sales area by running the report HRBCI_ATTRIBUTES_BUFFER_UPDATE in SA38

Answer: a, c, d

Explanation:

Erroneous BDOC messages are checked in CRM, **Not** in ECC.

In the above scenario, the following steps need to be followed:

1. Check if you have **generated** ECC org structure without errors through CRMC_R3_ORG_GENERATE.

2. If yes, go to tcode- PPOMA_CRM, select your SALES ORG go to ATTRIBUTES Tab - Assign the distribution channels and divisions manually if they are not available. Select the Object permitted in determination check box. (Refer Screenshots below)

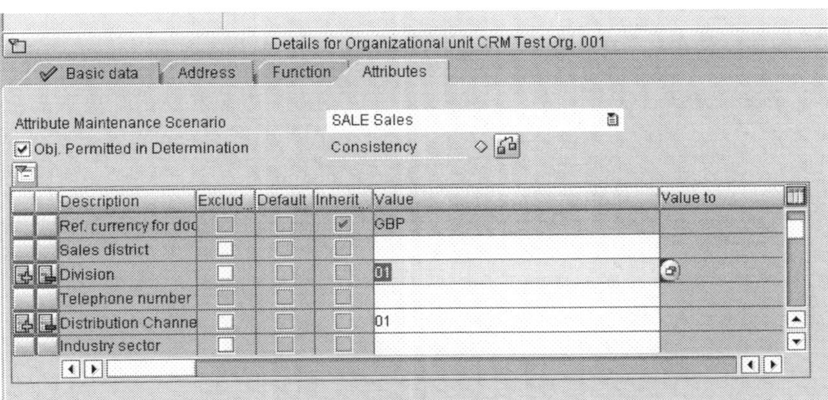

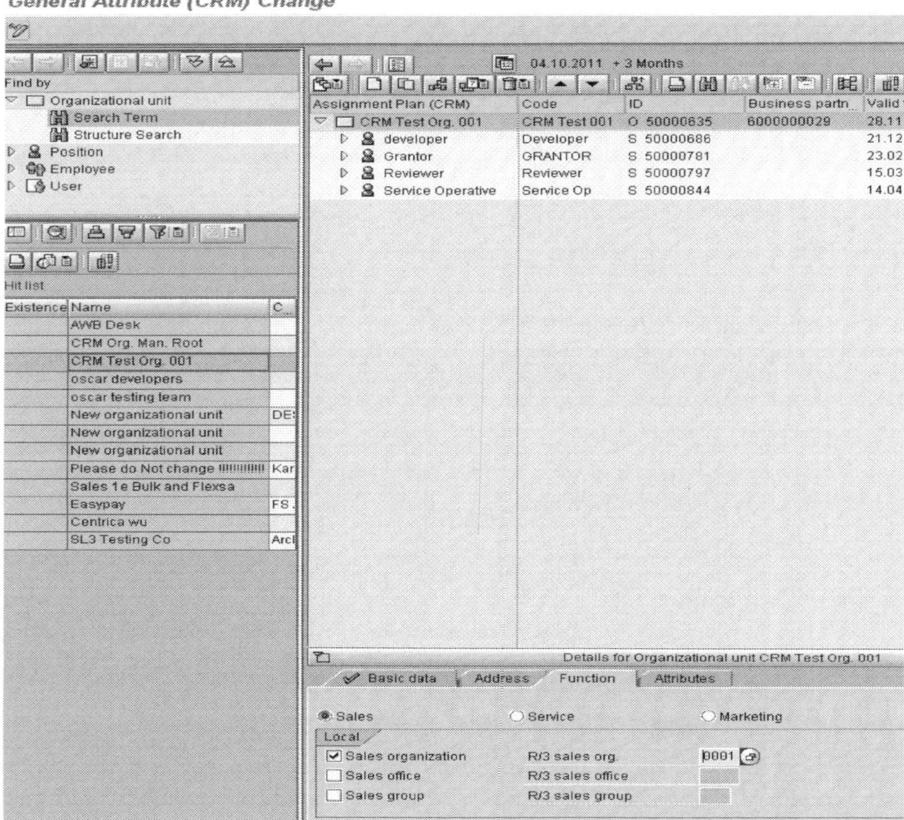

3. Run the tcode - CRMD_DOWNLOAD_SB, Go to table SMOTVKOV and check if the entries match after running the above tcode.

4. Run the report CRM_MKTBP_ZCACL_UPDATE_30 in SA38.

5. Run the report CRM_ORG_INDEX_CREATE in SA38 for values 'O' & 'S'. (Organization and Position)

6. Create buffer for sales area by running the report HRBCI_ATTRIBUTES_BUFFER_UPDATE in SA38

7. Now download object DNL_CUST_S_AREA through R3AS and check for the sales area.

Q2. You wish to monitor the initial load from SAP ERP to SAP CRM, which of the following transactions may be considered? (More than one option is correct)

a. Outbound Queue Scheduler (Transaction SMQS)

b. Middleware trace (Transaction SMWT)

c. BDoc details (SMW01)

d. Administration Console (SMOEAC)

Answer: a, b, c

Explanation:

The administration Console (in CRM) is used to **set up the Replication** with ERP by defining sites etc.

It is **not** used for monitoring.

The following tools are available for Monitoring Initial Load from ERP to CRM.

Monitoring tools:

- **Monitoring Initial Load:** R3AM1
- **qRFC-Monitoring:**
  - **Outbound Queue Scheduler:** SMQS
  - **Outbound Queue:** SMQ1
  - **Inbound Queue Scheduler:** SMQR
  - **Inbound Queue:** SMQ2
- **BDoc Monitoring:**
  - BDoc Datails: SMW01
  - BDoc Summary: SMW02
- **Middleware Trace:** SMWT
- **Middleware Monitoring Cockpit:** SMWP

Q3. With reference to SAP Middleware, which of the following statements are true?

(More than one option is correct)

a. The bi-directional qRFC technology is used.

b. Data is replicated to SAP ERP using ERP Adapters.

c. CRM uses the CSA* queues to validate data before subsequent processing.

d. Mobile Clients can be connected to CRM either permanently or temporarily

Answer: a, c, d

Explanation:

Data Exchange between CRM and ERP happens mainly via the CRM middleware. A **plug-in** installed on the ERP system acts like the ERP adapter, supporting data communication between the two systems.

The following are some of the **Key steps** needed for setting up Middleware:

- Define RFC destinations.

In SAP Customer Relationship Management (SAP CRM), create the RFC connection from SAP CRM to SAP ERP (transaction SM59):

type: 'ABAP Connections'. Use a suitable ERP user, such as CRMOLTP.

In SAP ERP, create the RFC connection from SAP ERP to SAP CRM (transaction SM59):

type: 'ABAP Connections'. Use a suitable CRM user, such as RFC.

-SAP CRM: **Register the CSA* queues in the qRFC monitor.**

Check whether queues with the name CSABUPA* (or CSA*) and R3A* exist.

-SAP CRM: **Create sites and subscriptions** for data distribution using the middleware (transaction SMOEAC).

Q4. With reference to data transfer of customizing data from ERP, to CRM, you may define filter criteria in CRM. These filter criteria can be automatically synchronized with ERP.

a. True
b. False

Answer : a

Explanation:

Saving a filter setting in CRM triggers the automatic transfer to the Plug-In in R/3.

Refer screenshot below.

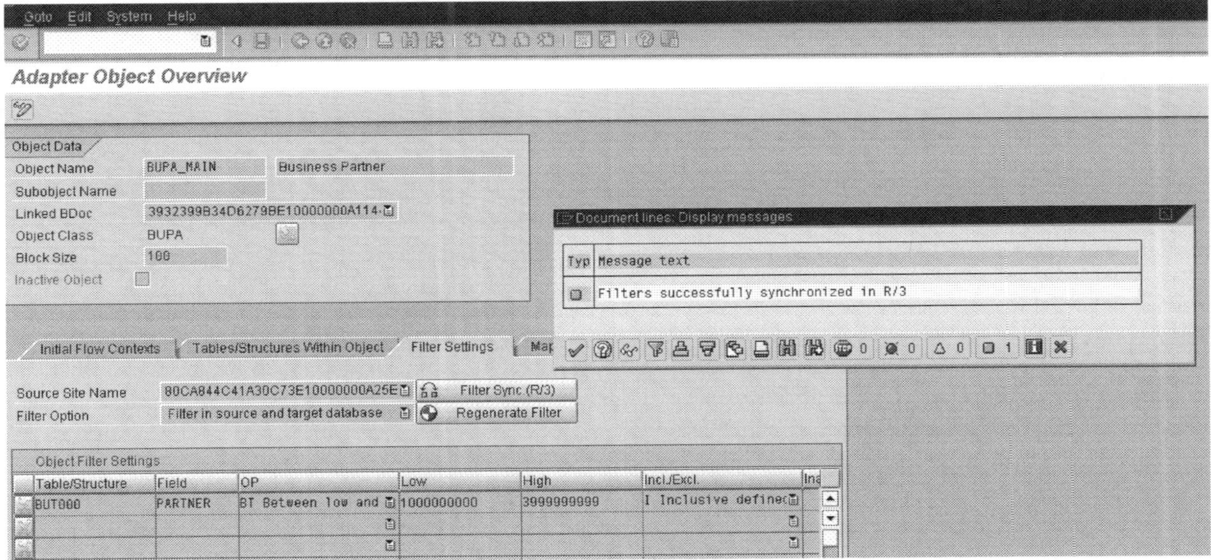

Q5. CRM uses BDocs for communication, rather than IDocs. Some of the key features that BDocs offer are: (More than one option is correct)

a. Data that belongs together is transported in one single unit.

b. The load is less as only the 'delta' is transported.

c. BDOCs are capable of using tRFC or qRFC giving additional flexibility.

d. BDOCs can be used in CRM, as well as in ALE & EDI

Answer: a, b, c

Explanation:

BDocs are used only in CRM and NOT in ALE or EDI.

The following table lists the differences between Business Document (BDoc) messages and Intermediate Document (IDoc) messages.

BDoc Messages	IDoc Messages
Use transactional RFC or queued RFC	Use transactional RFC
Are used in CRM	Are used in ALE and EDI
Are based on a BDoc type	Are based on an IDoc type
Contain delta field values	Contain all the field values

Q6. Which of the following statements are true? (More than one option is correct)

a. One BDOC type can be associated with only one Replication Object.

b. One Publication can be associated with multiple BDOCs

c. Once subscription can be associated with One Publication only

Answer: a, c

Explanation:

The diagram below shows the relationship between BDoc Type, Replication Object, Publication and Subscription.

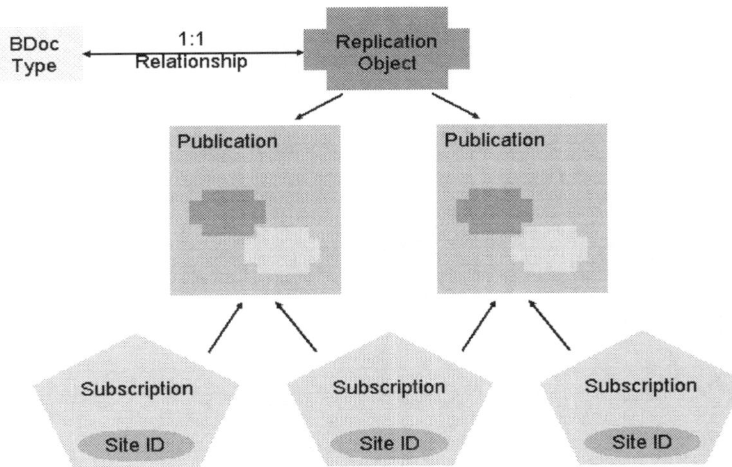

One single replication object is generated from a BDoc type, using the administration console.

Replication objects are grouped together logically in publications. A publication makes one or more replication objects available for replication. Sites can then subscribe to one or more publications, to receive the data relevant for their work. In a mobile scenario, employees can be assigned to the company and organizations assigned to a site.

Q7. Data across different components of an SAP landscape needs to be consistent. With reference to this, which of the following statements are true? (More than one option is correct)

a. The Data Integrity Manager (DIMa) can be used to repair inconsistent customizing settings between CRM and R/3 backends.

b. Objects may be compared at Header or Item level.

c. DIMa cannot be used in a mobile scenario.

Answer : a, b

Explanation:

The Data Integrity Manager (DIMa) helps you detect and repair nconsistencies between objects across components within the SAP CRM system landscape.

Data comparisons are always carried out for the CRM database and an R/3 backend database, or between a CRM database and a **consolidated database used for mobile clients**.

Header compare allows you to check is an object exists in both databases.

Detail compare compares all the data of the object instance.

The figure below shows how to create a DIMa instance.

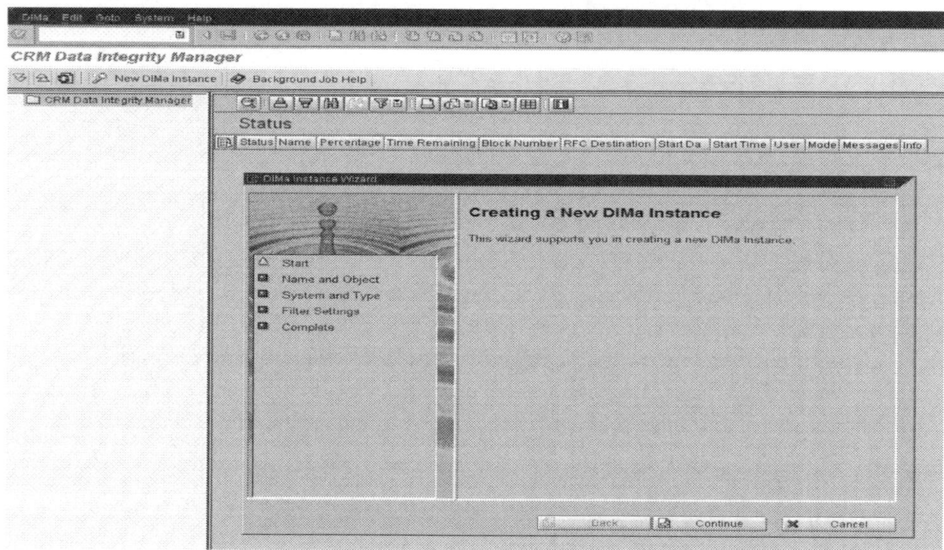

Q8. The CRM WebClient application can be modified in several ways.

With reference to the above, which of the following statements are true? (More than one option is correct)

a. If you want to change field labels across multiple views, you can use the design layer to consolidate the field changes.

b. You can use the UI Configuration Tool to adapt the user interface of SAP CRM to your company's specific requirements. You can access the UI Configuration Tool in SAP GUI and in the CRM WebClient UI.

c. You cannot change the standard access sequence that is used to determine configurations.

Answer : a, b

Explanation:

- If you want to change field labels across multiple views, you can use the design layer to consolidate the field changes. You define these settings in Customizing under *Customer Relationship Management →UI Framework →UI Framework Definition →Design Layer* .

  You can use the UI Configuration Tool to adapt the user interface of SAP CRM to your company's specific requirements. You can access the UI Configuration Tool in SAP GUI and in the CRM WebClient UI.

- If you want to change customer-specific fields that were created with the Easy Enhancement Workbench (EEW), and are contained in views, you can do so by using the UI Configuration Tool in the same way as with standard fields. You define your own fields in Customizing under *Customer Relationship Management →CRM Cross-Application Components →Easy Enhancement Workbench* .

Configuration Access Sequence

You can change the standard access sequence that is used to determine configurations. The actual configuration that is used for a certain configurable view is determined on the basis of a search key and the available configurations that exist for a specific view. The configuration can either be a standard SAP configuration or a customer-specific configuration.

To use your own access sequence, you need to implement the Business Add-In (BAdI) BSP_DLC_ACCESS_ENHANCEMENT in Customizing for Customer Relationship Management, by choosing UI Framework UI Framework Definition Business Add-Ins (BAdIs) Define Configuration Access BAdI: Configuration Access Determination .

Q9. As an application consultant, one of your tasks is to configure CRM Business Roles.

Which of the following are Relationships of Business Roles: (More than one option is correct)

a. Business Role is related to the Navigation Bar Profile
b. Business Role is related to the Organization Model
c. Business Role is related to the authorization profile
d. Business Role is related to Data Replication

Answer: a, b, c

Explanation:

A business role depends on the following relationships:

To the **navigation bar profile** in which you define all links that are available on the different work center pages, on the **Home page**, on **report pages** and in **direct link groups**. To define the links, use the IMG activity Define Navigation Bar Profile.

In the IMG activity Define Business Role, you can change or hide links and work centers that are defined in the navigation bar profile assigned to a business role.

To the **organizational unit** in the organizational model. To assign organizational units to users, use the IMG activity Define Organizational Assignment.

The organizational model is also used to assign business roles to users. Via the same organizational unit, user and business role are directly related.

To the **authorization role** via the PFCG role defined in the IMG activity Define Authorization Role.

Assignment of Users to Business Roles

You can assign a user to a business role by using one of the following options:

Assign user and business role to the same organizational unit. This is the recommended approach.

Assign a user to the authorization role, which is assigned to the business role, as used in Partner Channel Management.

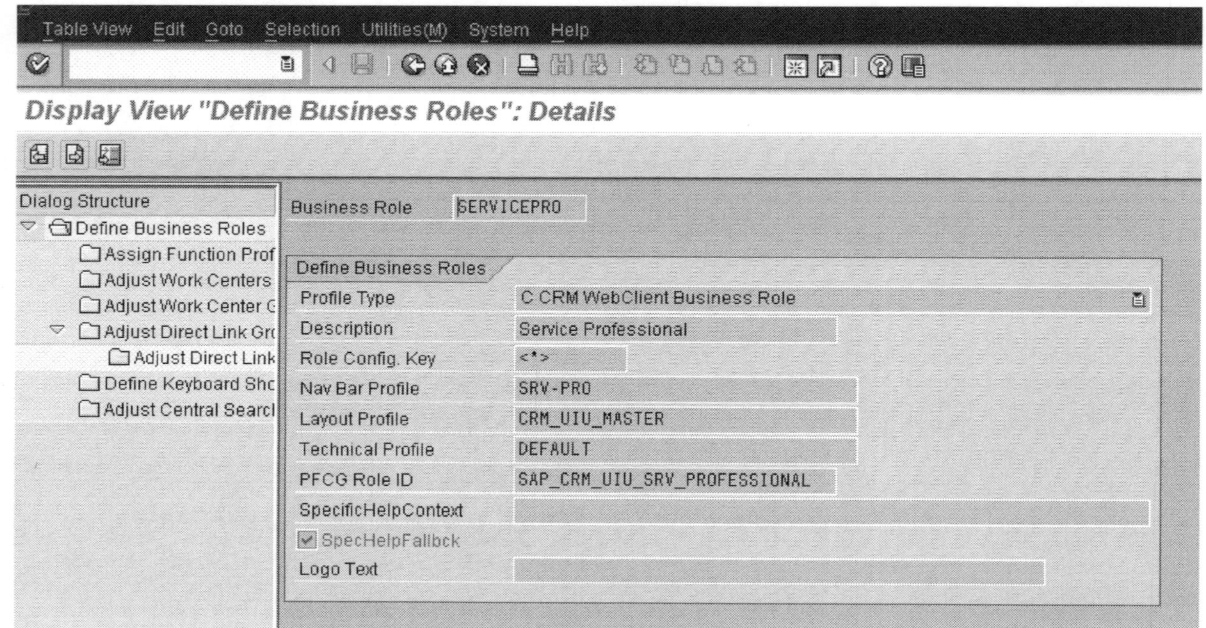

Business Role is **NOT** related to data replication.

Q10.The navigation bar profile defines the content that is displayed in the navigation bar. It is assigned to a business role in Customizing. Which of the following are assigned directly to the Navigation Bar Profile? (More than one option is correct)

a. Work Centers
b. Direct Link Group
c. Logical Links

Answer: a, b

Explanation:

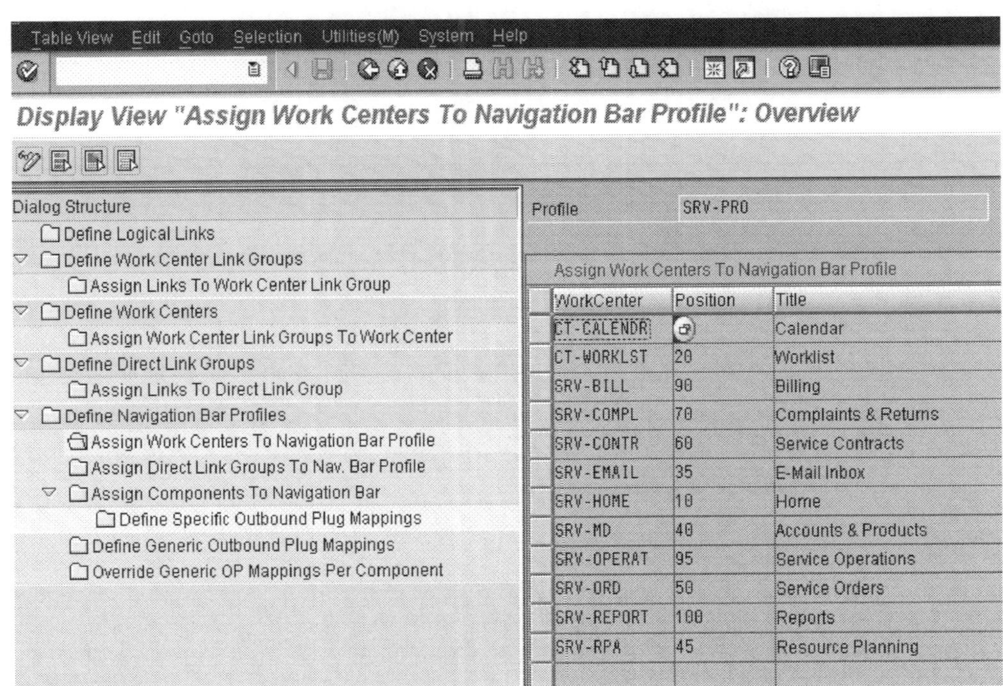

The following are **Key** steps for setting up a Navigation Bar Profile

1. Create a navigation bar profile. Determine the following data:

Navigation bar profile

Meaningful description

Default link ID

The default link ID for business roles is Home.

2. Assign work centers to the profile.

Work centers are reusable parts that can be used in many different profiles.

3. Assign direct link groups to the profile.

Direct link groups are reusable parts that can be used in many different profiles.

4. Assign components to the profile.

You must configure all components that you want to make available in your navigation bar profile.

5. Define the generic outbound plug (OP) mappings.

Q11. A logical link can be assigned to work centers, direct link groups, or work center pages. Which types of logical links are possible? (More than one option is correct)

a. Work Center
b. BOR Object
c. Launch Transaction
d. BI Report

Answer : a, c, d

Explanation:

The diagram below is self explanatory.

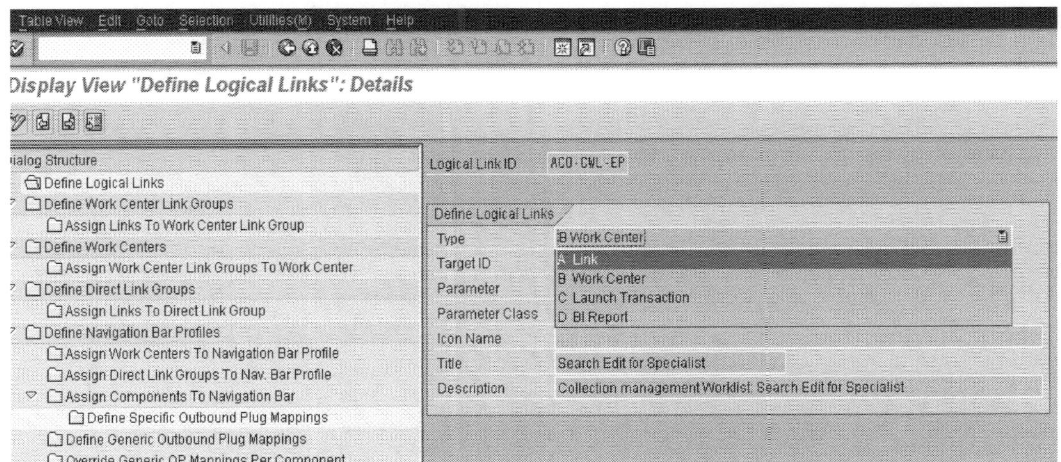

Q12. The Transaction Launcher function allows agents to access business transactions directly from the IC WebClient. The main benefit of using launch transactions is to save agents from logging into multiple systems and repeating data entry.Which of the following can be launched by a transaction launcher? (More than one option is correct)

a. URLs

b. BSPs

c. BOR transactions

Answer: a, b, c

Explanation:

You can use this function to launch:

Uniform Resource Locators (URLs)

Business Server Pages (BSPs) of other systems

Business Object Repository (BOR) transactions

To launch BSPs and BOR transactions, you have defined the logical system. You have mapped this logical system with transaction Transaction Launcher Logical Systems (CRMS_IC_CROSS_SYS).

You need to map the logical system to the current target logical system and have defined the SAP Internet Transaction Server (ITS) to be used. This mapped logical system is then used in the transaction launcher.

To launch BOR transactions in SAP ERP, you have to define the following:

The RFC system setup with transaction RFC Destinations (SM59)

The logical system with transaction Maintaining Logical Systems (BD54)

To launch URLs, you have defined the URLs in a URL repository. You have defined the URL in view CRMV_IC_LTX_URL, which is accessible via transaction Maintain Table Views (SM30). If you want to call sap.com for example, you need to define an URL with the ID SAP and enter the complete URL, that is, http://www.sap.com. This ID is then used in the transaction launcher.

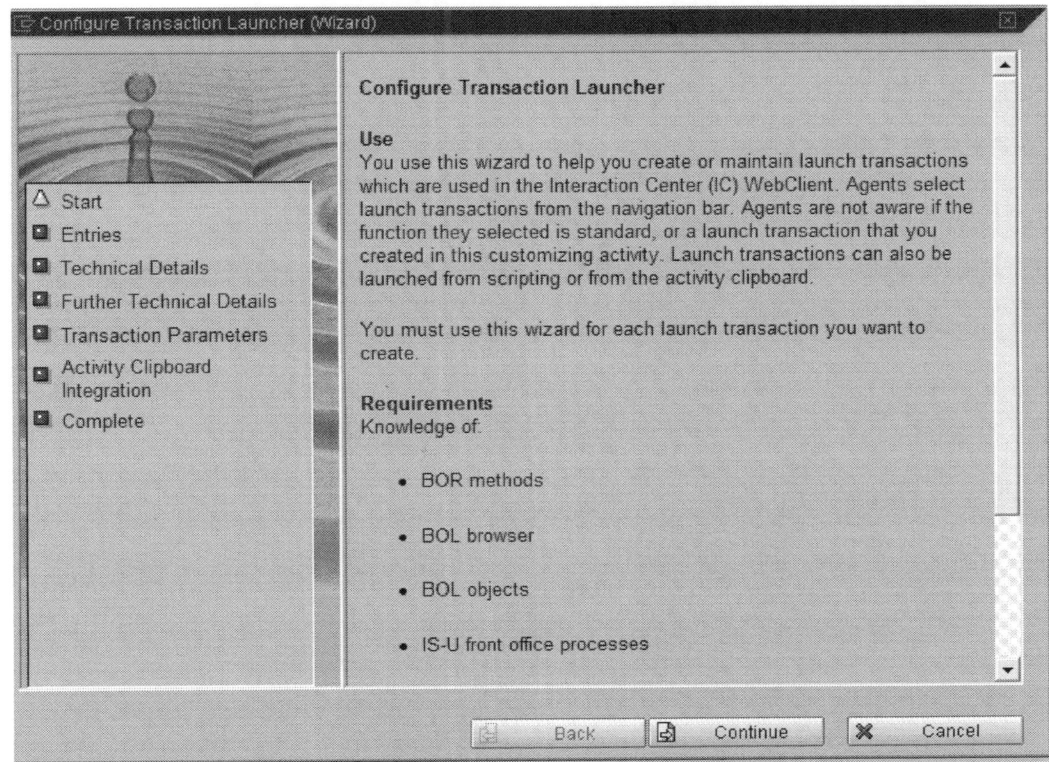
Configure Transaction Launcher (Wizard)
Start
Entries
Technical Details
Further Technical Details
Transaction Parameters
Activity Clipboard Integration
Complete
Configure Transaction Launcher
Use
You use this wizard to help you create or maintain launch transactions which are used in the Interaction Center (IC) WebClient. Agents select launch transactions from the navigation bar. Agents are not aware if the function they selected is standard, or a launch transaction that you created in this customizing activity. Launch transactions can also be launched from scripting or from the activity clipboard.
You must use this wizard for each launch transaction you want to create.
Requirements
Knowledge of:
BOR methods
BOL browser
BOL objects
IS-U front office processes
Back
Continue
Cancel

Q13. The role configuration key can be defined in Customizing, and assigned to a business role. With this parameter, it is possible to create business-role-dependent configurations. At runtime, this parameter is automatically determined by the business role with which the user is logged on.

a. True

b. False

Answer : a

Explanation:

The statement is true. The figures below show how to set up the Role Configuration Key.

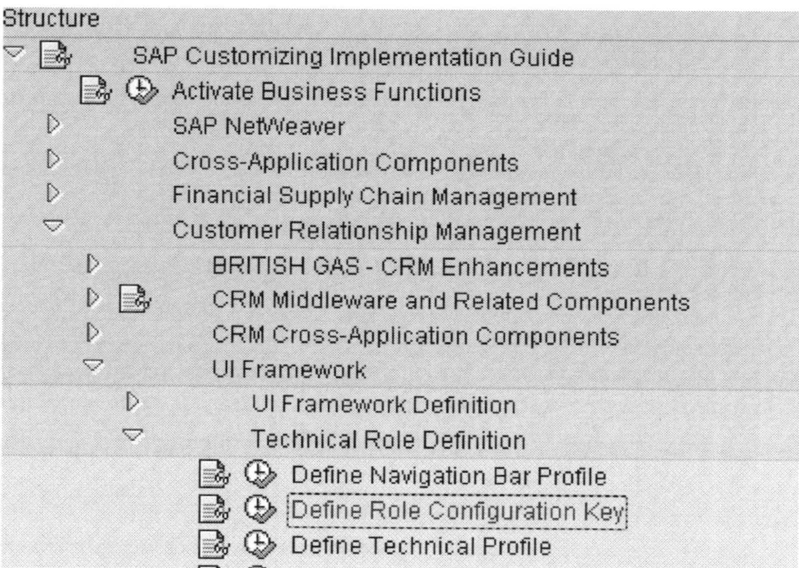

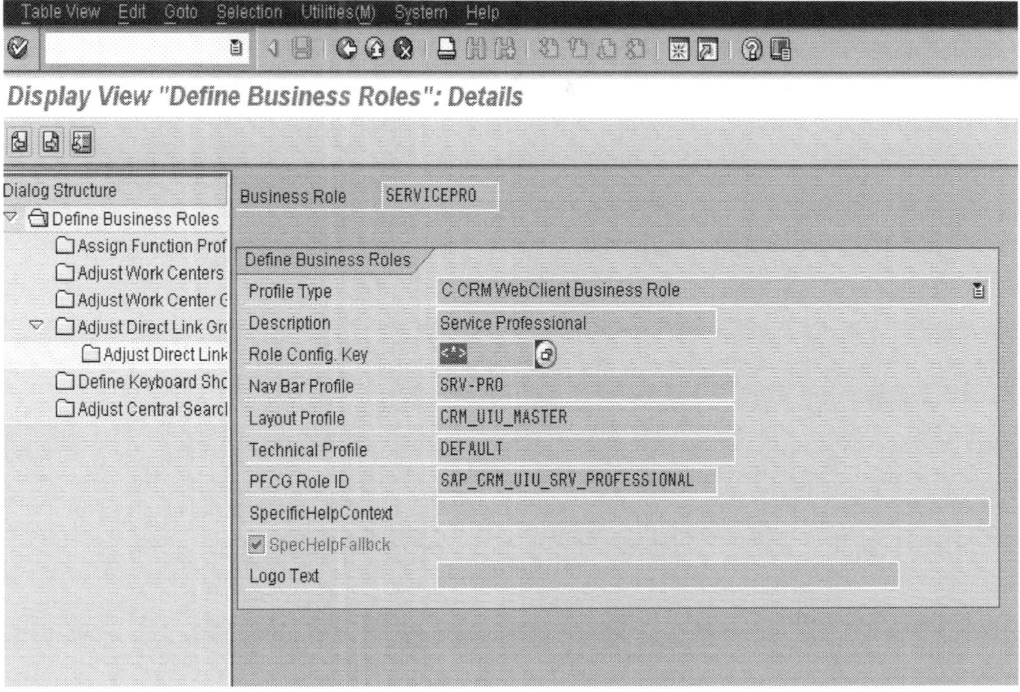
Table View Edit Goto Selection Utilities(M) System Help
Display View "Define Business Roles": Details
Dialog Structure
Define Business Roles
Assign Function Prof
Adjust Work Centers
Adjust Work Center G
Adjust Direct Link Gr
Adjust Direct Link
Define Keyboard Shc
Adjust Central Searcl
Business Role SERVICEPRO
Define Business Roles
Profile Type C CRM WebClient Business Role
Description Service Professional
Role Config. Key <*>
Nav Bar Profile SRV-PRO
Layout Profile CRM_UIU_MASTER
Technical Profile DEFAULT
PFCG Role ID SAP_CRM_UIU_SRV_PROFESSIONAL
SpecificHelpContext
SpecHelpFallbck
Logo Text

Q14. When processing a business transaction, certain organizational data is mandatory depending on the transaction type. The Organization data can be determined in different ways.

Which of the following are ways to determine the Organizational data?(More than one option is correct)

a. Manual determination
b. Automatic determination
c. Semi-automatic determination

Answer: a, b

Explanation:

In SAP CRM you have the following options for determining organizational data in the transaction. You can set these in Customizing depending on the transaction type:

- **no determination**

  In this case, enter the organizational data (for example, sales area) manually in the transaction.

1. You have created an organizational data profile in Customizing, in which *no* determination rules have been entered.
2. You have assigned this organizational data profile to the required transaction type.

- **automatic determination**

  The system determines organizational data using the data available in the transaction, for example, the business partner number, region, product, or using the user assignments for the organizational unit (using the position).

1. You have created a determination rule in Customizing for each determination path with the corresponding rule type.
2. You have defined one or two determination rules in the organizational data profile for evaluating the organizational data profile of a transaction.
3. You have assigned the organizational data profile to a transaction type.

You carry out the settings in Customizing for CRM. Choose *Master Data →Organizational Management →Organizational Data Determination*.

Q15. With reference to the Organizational Data Profile, which of the following statements are true? (More than one option is correct)

a. If you define two determination rules in the organizational data profile, the system creates the intersection from the resulting quantity of the two rule resolutions.

b. There is no individual organizational data determination at item level.

c. An organizational unit in the *Sales scenario* can have different attributes with different values to an organizational unit in the *Service scenario*.

d. The system cannot determine more than one responsible org unit.

Answer : a, b, c, d

Explanation:

When determining organizational data, the system takes the organizational data profile defined in Customizing and the determination rules from this profile.

Rule type Responsibilities

Rule type Organizational Model

The basic rule types Organizational Data and Function Module are available in CRM, but to use them you must have ABAP/4 knowledge.

Defining rules using organizational data

Defining rules using function to be executed

If you define two determination rules in the organizational data profile, the system creates the intersection from the resulting quantity of the two rule resolutions.

Determining organizational data can differ according to the scenario, because an organizational unit in the *Sales scenario* can have **different attributes with different values** to an organizational unit in the *Service scenario*.

Organizational data at item level

If you do not use a header division in business transactions, the *Division* attribute only exists at item level. In this case the division is derived from the product and all of the organizational data at item level of a transaction, except for the division, may not differ from that in the header. There is therefore no individual organizational data determination at item level. The following options for organizational data at item level are possible. You can set these in Customizing. They are dependent on the item category.

Settings for Organizational Data at Item Level

Organizational data at item level	Settings you must make in Customizing
Without header division: The organizational data is copied from the document header. The division is derived from the product.	Assign an organizational data profile without a determination rule to the item category.
With header division: The organizational data is copied from the document header. The division is derived from the document header.	Assign an organizational data profile without a determination rule to the item category.
There is no organizational data at item level (no *organizational data* screen)	Do not assign the organizational data profile to the item category.

If the system determines more than one responsible organizational unit or determines several attribute values for the responsible organizational unit, a **selection screen** appears.

Q16. Org data can be maintained in ECC as well as in CRM. In this context, which of the following statements are true. (More than one option is correct)

a. Distribution Channel is mandatory in ECC, but not mandatory in CRM

b. Division is mandatory in ECC, but not mandatory in CRM

c. Sales Org is mandatory in ECC, but not mandatory in CRM

Answer: a, b, c

Explanation:

The following table outlines the Key differences between Org data determination in ECC & CRM.

Key Differences

Function / Feature	In SAP ECC (SD)	In SAP CRM
General	You maintain the sales organization in Customizing under Organization Settings. You maintain the organizational plan for HR and Workflow independently in *Business Management* (Basis).	You maintain the organizational model once for all applications in CRM. Scenario-specific data in the structure is assigned by attributes to the organizational units. These attributes are passed onto subordinate organizational units.
	Organizational data in Sales and Distribution is static, changes in organizational data result in major changes in Customizing.	Organizational models can be maintained and adapted dynamically.
	Responsibilities are proposed from the sales area-related data from the customer master	Responsibilities are defined independently from the business partner master and are determined, if required, from the organizational model.
Sales area	when creating a sales document • entered manually or • determined using the customer master for the	when creating a transaction document • entered manually or • determined using organizational

Function / Feature	In SAP ECC (SD)	In SAP CRM
	sold-to party	data determination
		In Customizing you set whether you wish to have a division at header level of a document in the sales area. If you decide not to use a header division you need to use a dummy division (see SAP ECC dummy division). A business partner master must therefore have data for at least one sales area with an "empty"division, so that it can be used at the header level of documents
Distribution chain (sales organization and distribution channel)	is mandatory in sales documents	can be flagged as mandatory in Customizing (org. data profile) It is recommended that you flag the distribution chain as mandatory for sales documents
Sales organization	only one sales organization can occur in a sales document. This organization is responsible for the processing of the business transaction.	The organizational unit responsible for the document need not be a sales organization. It can also be, for example, a sales office. You can assign business partners directly to the sales organization
Distribution Channel	is an organizational object	is not an independent object. It is an attribute that can be assigned to an organizational unit.
	is defined in Customizing	can be replicated from the SAP ECC (during the initial download), or, can be defined in SAP CRM in Customizing.
Division	must be used. If a company does not use division schedule lines, a general division ("cross-division") must be set up and used.	Use of the division can be switched off throughout the system
	is defined in Customizing	can be replicated from SAP ECC (during the

Function / Feature	In SAP ECC (SD)	In SAP CRM
		initial download), or, can be redefined in SAP CRM in Customizing.
	is an organizational object can be assigned to only one distribution chain and not to a sales organization.	The division is not an organizational unit, but an attribute. Several divisions can be assigned to a sales organization independent of the distribution channel.
	Sales document has a sales area, therefore also a division at header level (header division).	You set in Customizing whether there is a header division. If you do not use a header division, the division only exists at item level and is always derived from the product. If you do use a header division, the header division is valid for the entire business transaction.
Sales office	is assigned to a sales area	The sales office can be directly assigned to a sales organization.
	can be assigned to a customer in the customer master.	Business partners and other attributes (for example, postal code area) can be assigned to the sales office, independent of the sales area.
Sales group	can be assigned in the sales data of the customer master to a customer as a responsible group	Business partners and other attributes can be assigned to the sales group.
	Assignment of an employee to the sales group, sales office and/or sales organization takes place in personnel master via Info type 900, an employee can only be assigned to one organizational unit (sales group)	Assignment of employees to an organizational unit using positions in the organizational model This makes it possible to assign an employee to different positions and organizational units. It is recommended you assign only one employee to a position, if you are also using CRM Territory Management.
Service organization	displayed as maintenance planning plant	own entity, comparable with sales organization in Sales scenario, is responsible

Function / Feature	In SAP ECC (SD)	In SAP CRM
		for processing service transactions
Determination of employee responsible (ER)	via customer master for sold-to party (or another partner in accordance with partner determination procedure)	• via the sales area-dependent partner function Employee responsible in the BP master • via the BP relationship defined in the business partner master • via assignment in the organizational model
Organizational unit as business partner (cross-company)	not possible; a customer master record must be created for the organizational unit	possible; when creating an organizational unit, a business partner master (organization category) is automatically created.
Sales district (customer district)	is defined in the customer master and copied from there into the document	is assigned to an organizational unit in the organizational model as an attribute and, if required, is copied from the responsible organizational unit into the document.

SAP CRM Transactional Processing

1) Identify the component which describes the structure of CRM Business transactions?

a) Transaction Channels

b) Customizing header

c) Transaction determination procedure

d) Transaction Type

Answer: d.

Explanation:

A transaction type specifies the characteristics and attributes of a business transaction and the control attributes (for example, partner determination procedure, text determination procedure, status profile, organizational data profile). A transaction type controls the processing of a specific business transaction, for example a standard order.

A business transaction type is assigned to one business transaction category (for example, activity, opportunity, sales, and service). The business transaction category defines the business context in which a business transaction type can be used.

Business transaction category defines the business context in which a transaction type can be used (for example, service, sales, and activity). When you create a transaction type, one or several business transaction categories must be assigned to this transaction type. For example, the business transaction categories sales and activity are assigned to the transaction type standard order. This means that activity data can also be entered in this sales transaction.

The following graphic shows the process of the transaction type:

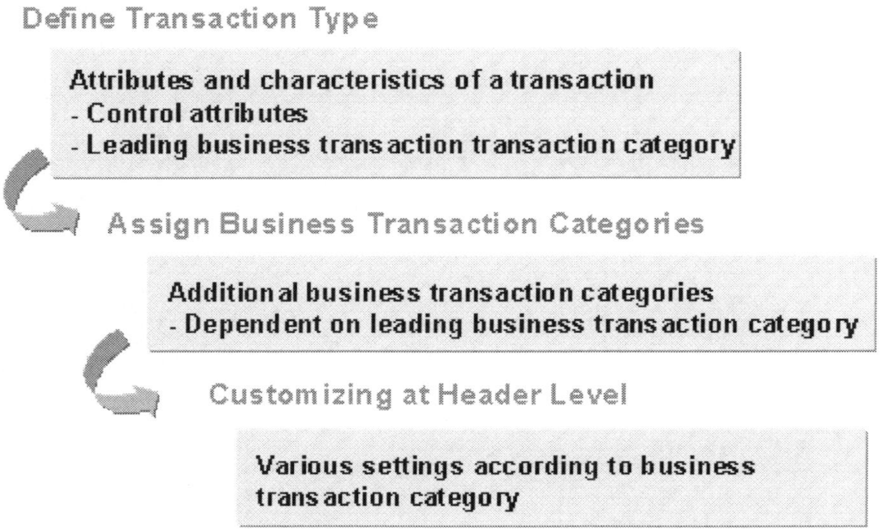

Define Transaction Type

Attributes and characteristics of a transaction
- Control attributes
- Leading business transaction transaction category

Assign Business Transaction Categories

Additional business transaction categories
- Dependent on leading business transaction category

Customizing at Header Level

Various settings according to business transaction category

2) Which of the following attributes are used for item category determination? (Choose more than one option)

a) Item Category Group

b) Transaction Type

c) Org Data Profile

d) Access sequence

Answer: a & b.

Explanation:

An item category specifies the characteristics and attributes of a transaction item, and controls the processing of an item. Item category determination is a function that determines the item category for CRM Billing using specified attributes of CRM business transactions. This service is mandatory for the billing process as the system uses it to control the transfer of billing relevant data to CRM Billing.

For example, the item category controls the type and scope of:

- Pricing
- Billing
- Delivery
- Inventory posting
- Transfer of requirements

For processing of business transactions, the system uses the item category group to determine the item category. From the item category group of the product and the current transaction type, the system determines the item category and enters it as default in the relevant transaction at item level.

You can make the relevant settings for item category determination in the Implementation Guide, under Customer Relationship Management ->Transactions->Basic Settings->Define Item Category Determination.

3) Which of the following can be used to record and update the information of products discussed with customer and feedback from the customer during the customer visit or telephone calls within the activity management?

a) Actions

b) Activity Journal

c) Product promotion list

d) Texts

Answer: b.

Explanation:

Activity Journal is used by sales employees during or after an activity to record all information gathered from a customer visit or telephone call. An activity journal may contain information on products discussed with the customer, samples given, feedback from the customer, or information on an upcoming event.

A pre-defined form used to define the item structures of information gathered from a customer visit or telephone call. An activity journal template type defines the item structures of an activity journal. The template type defines which fields are available for maintenance in an activity journal.

Validity criteria for the activity journal template type are defined by specifying transaction types, activity categories, and time periods. A template type must be assigned to a template in order to work with activity journals during activity processing.

The information recorded in the activity journal can also be used to:

- Analyze sales data, for example, the number of products distributed to the customer
- Track the progress of the sales team, for example, the number and type of discussions held with a business partner
- Detect possible problems, for example, any slow and non-moving products

Here is the graphical representation of the whole activity management:

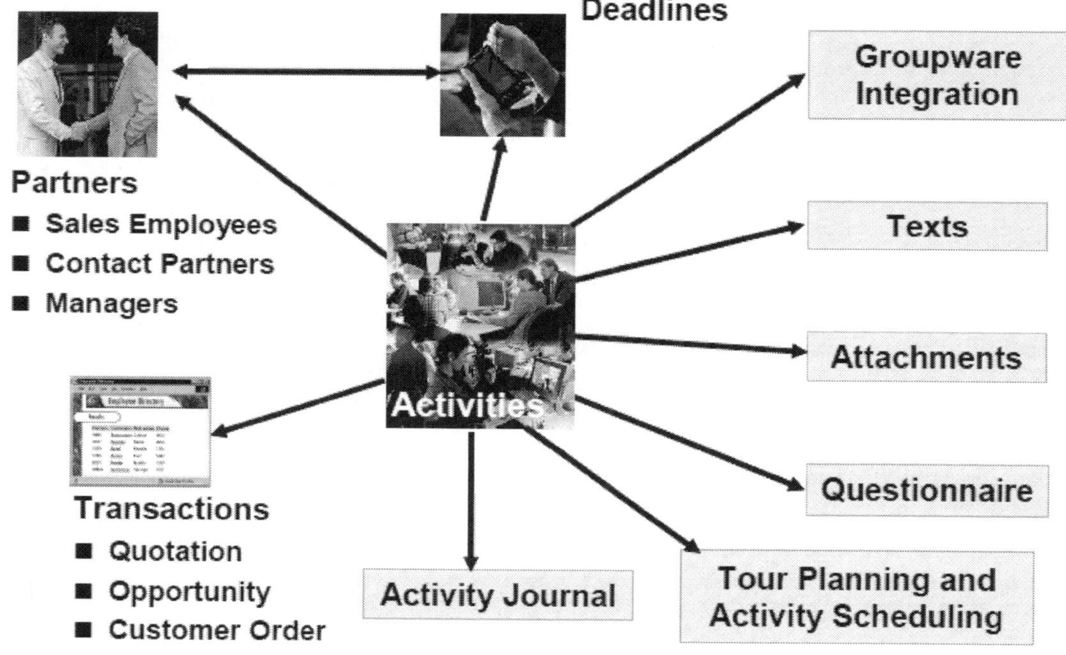

4) The Head of the department of your company asked the tool which is used to track all the activities created for each team member of his/her team. Which of the following tool do you recommend?

a) Activity Journal

b) Activity Monitor

c) Pipeline analysis

d) None of the above

Answer: b.

Explanation:

The Activity Monitor enables you to call up lists of all the activities that have been created in the system.

You can select activities for:

- **Yourself:** you are the employee assigned to the activity
- **Your team:** you are the head of a department and want to view activities created by or belonging to all employees in your team
- **Your colleagues:** you are a member of the team and want to view activities created by or belonging to employees in the same team
- **Specific business partners**

The Activity Monitor contains three selection variants:

- My incomplete activities
- Incomplete activities of my team
- Incomplete activities of my colleagues

You can access these variants directly from the CRM user menu under Activities.

The Activity Monitor displays activities according to the selection criteria you have chosen. The variants display all the incomplete business activities for the relevant partners. You can double-click on an activity in the list to go directly to the Activity Processing screen.

Activity Monitor can be called by choosing Activities-> Activity Monitor in the SAP Menu.

5) When a sales order is created with reference to quotation, which of the following options can be used as a copy controls? (Choose more than one option)

a) Copy controls of transaction types

b) Copy controls for Item category

c) Copy controls using BADI

d) Copy controls using partners

Answer: a, b & c.

Explanation:

Copy control is used to copy the information from one document to the follow on documents. You need to maintain the copy controls at header and item level so that you can create follow up documents such as quotations or orders.

You can use the below options for maintain copy controls:

- Using Transaction types
- Using Item Category
- Using BADI

We cannot use copy controls by partners.

6) Your customer wants to use a new business activity for capturing trade fair contacts that can be used as follow up documents for leads. Which of the following settings are mandatory to fulfil these requirements? (choose more than one option)

a) Define a transaction type for the Trade Fair contacts using a leading business category 'Business Activity'

b) Set up Copy control for source transaction type 'Lead' and target transaction type ' Trade fair contact'

c) Maintain Item Category determination for the trade fair contact.

d) Implement a BADI for copy control.

Answer: a, b & c.

Explanation:

A BADI implementation is optional if you need something that the standard system will not provide.

7) **Which of the following statements are true when you define a relation between Transaction type and Item Category? (Choose more than one option)**

   a) A transaction type contains all relevant item categories

   b) An item category can be linked to only one transaction type.

   c) An item category can contain other item categories

   d) A transaction type may have no item category determination

Answer: c & d.

Explanation:

A transaction type specifies the characteristics and attributes of a business transaction and the control attributes (for example, partner determination procedure, text determination procedure, status profile, organizational data profile). A transaction type controls the processing of a specific business transaction, for example a standard order.

An item category specifies the characteristics and attributes of a transaction item, and controls the processing of an item.

A higher level Item category can have lower level item categories. This can be customized in Business transactions. An item category specifies the characteristics and attributes of a transaction item, and controls the processing of an item. Item Category may not be needed for the transaction types like activity or a task.

8) **Text data are maintained at header or item level in the Business transactions. Which of the following determines the texts at each Business transaction?**

   a) Text profile

b) Text Determination procedure

c) Notes assignment profile

d) Text type

Answer: b.

Explanation:

Text Determination procedure is used to determine the text at each business transaction. The steps in the procedure are as follows:

- Select a text object and define the rules for text determination for this object
- Define the permitted **text types** for every text object
- Define the **access sequences** . This way, you define how the SAP System should determine the texts for a text type.
- Group the text types together in determination procedures.
- Allocate the text determination procedures so that a procedure applies to the following criteria in each case
    - **account group** customer
    - sales & distribution **document type**
    - **item category**

9) The Business partner model in CRM controls business partner roles which classify the account according to their business function. Which of the following statement is true for business partner roles?

a) The business partner role of an account determines the number range that will be used

b) The business partner role describes the business relevant connection between two accounts or contacts

c) The business partner role has no influence on data exchange between SAP CRM and SAP ERP

d) All of the above

Answer: a

Explanation:

During business partner creation, the number assignment is determined by a 'Grouping'. When creating a business partner, internal number assignment is the default. If you want to use external number assignment instead, choose the relevant grouping and enter the external number.

10) Partner determination procedures control which of the following? (Choose more than one option)

a) Which internal business partners should be included in a business transaction
b) Which external business partners should be included in a business transaction
c) Which business partners are related to which other business partners
d) Which business partners/partner functions are mandatory

Answer: a, b, d

Explanation:

- Partner determination controls business partner processing in transaction processing.
- All transactions in CRM involve business partners. Partner processing includes partner determination procedure, System automatically finds and enters partners in transactions using the procedure.

Partner Processing

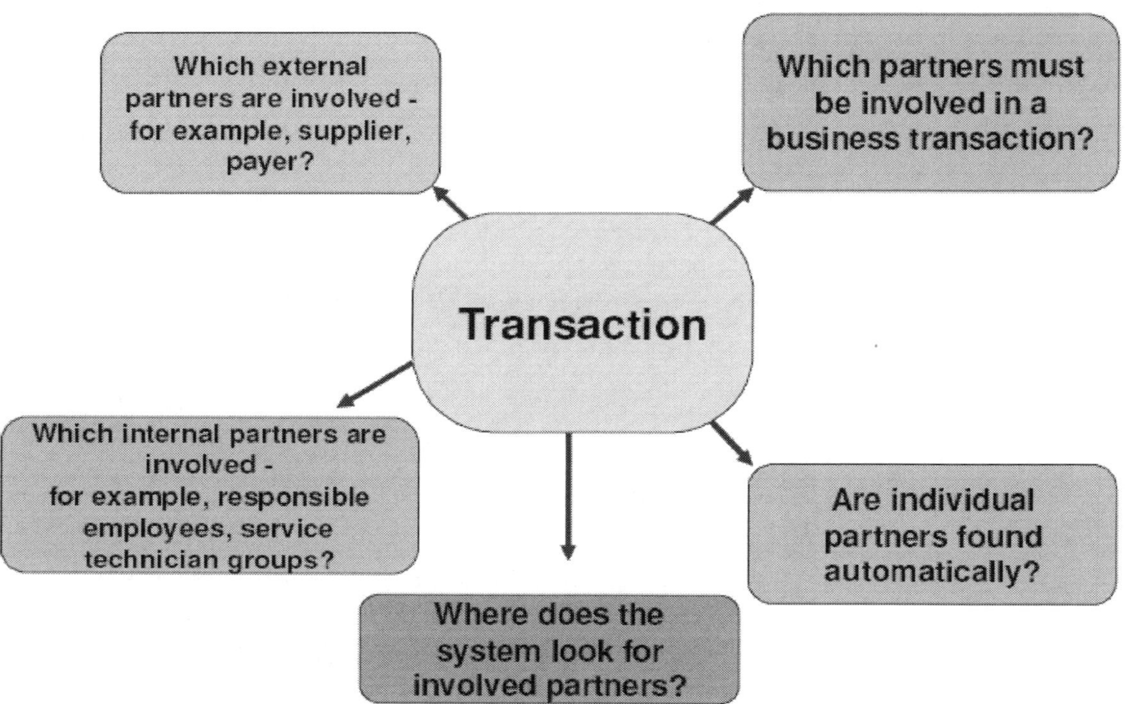

11) Partner determination procedure assigned to a transaction type must be same as the partner determination procedure assigned to an item category. Choose true or false.

a) True
b) False

Answer: b

Explanation:

In a transaction, partners can be determined at both header and item level.

It is possible that different partners are determined at header and item levels. Hence it is not required to have the same partner determination procedure at header and item levels.

12) Which of the following is correct?

a) Partner functions consist of partner function categories
b) Partner functions can use a lock to restrict source partner being determined for a partner function
c) Access sequence consists of partner functions
d) Partner function categories are freely definable

Answer: b

Explanation:

Partner function categories are predefined “classifications” and are assigned partner functions. The system uses these categories to identify and work with partner functions.

Lock specifies whether the source partner for a partner determination is added to the result list of that determination.

For example, if the lock field is set for the contact person partner function, the sold-to-party is not determined as its own contact person in a sales transaction. If, on the other hand, the lock field is set, the sold-to party can also appear as the contact person function in the transaction.

Partner Function Categories and Partner Functions

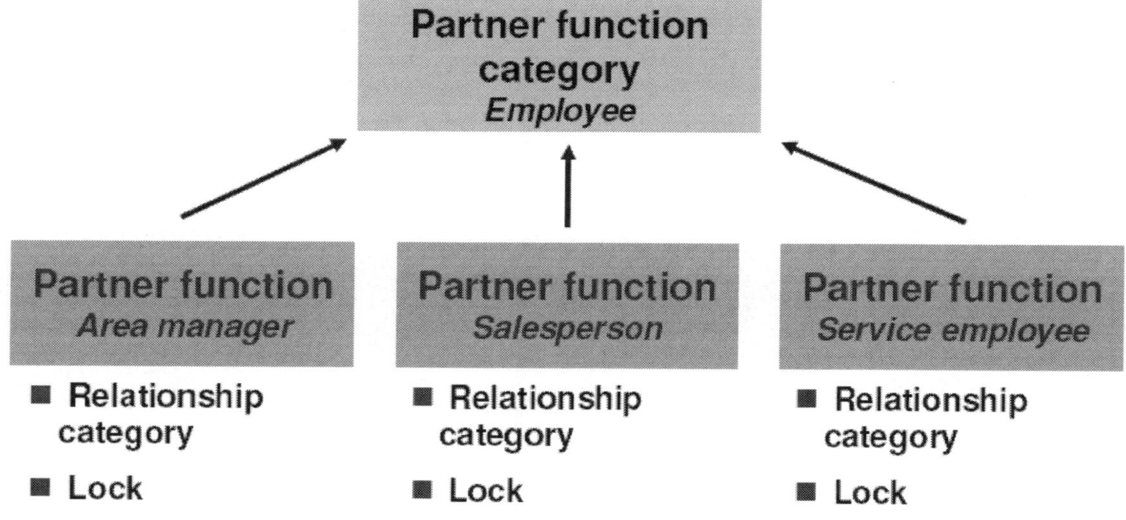

Partner functions are freely definable.
Partner function categories are predefined.

13) Which of the following are incorrect about partner determination procedure?

a) They can have a partner function with no assigned access sequence
b) They can set minimum and maximum number of partners for a partner function
c) They have to allow all available partner functions in CRM to be used in a transaction type
d) They can influence the calendar maintenance

Answer: c

Explanation:

You can choose a range of partner functions and then select a setting that limits the visibility of partner functions.

To prevent every partner function that is defined in the system and corresponding partners from being included in transactions, make the setting ***Permitted Functions = Only Functions Assigned in Procedure***.

14) In account management within CRM, by which of the following objects is the number assignment during account creation determined?

a) Account Type
b) Grouping
c) Role
d) All of the above

Answer: b

Explanation:

The number range in CRM is determined solely by Groupings. You can define groupings in customizing. This means that a grouping is automatically selected when you create a business partner.

15) Which assignments in customizing can be implemented when setting up Organization data determination in business transaction?

a) An organization data profile has to be assigned to the transaction type
b) A determination rule has to be assigned to transaction type
c) For determination rule type 'Org Model', responsibilities have to be assigned directly in the rule
d) All of the above

Answer: a

Explanation:

To determine the organizational data in a transaction, the system reads the organizational data profile that was assigned to the transaction type used in customizing.

A determination rule is derived from this organization data profile. In SAP CRM, there are two types of determination rule for determining the responsible organizational units:

- Organizational model

- Responsibilities

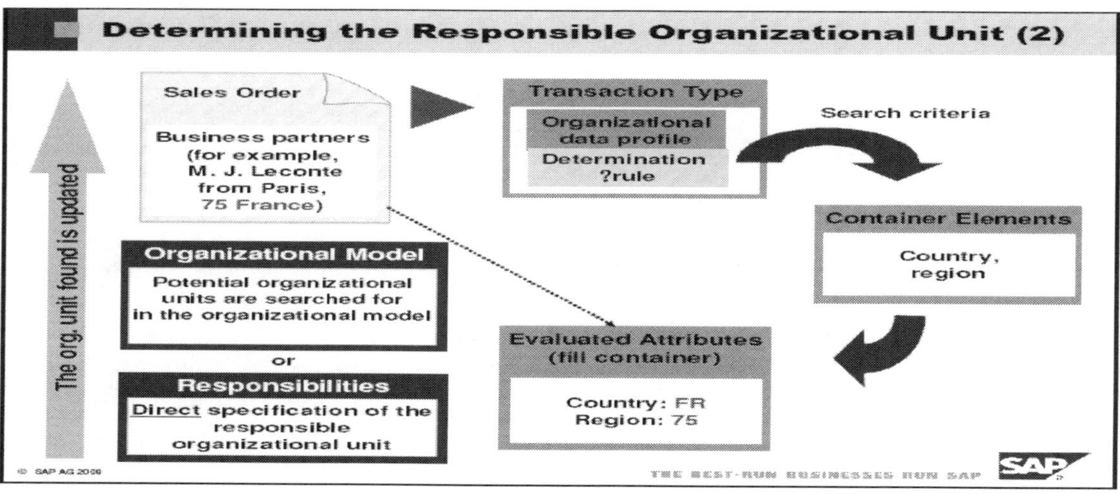

16) **Account classification is used to classify your account according to any criteria you choose. In that context, which of the following statement is correct?**

a) Account classification influences the header fields that are displayed within an account
b) Classification categories are fixed and cannot be enhanced
c) To each classification category, any number of criteria and attributes can be assigned
d) To each classification category, a fixed number of criteria and any number of attributes can be assigned

Answer: d

Explanation:

You can use account classification to classify your accounts according to any criteria. The required criteria can be combined in any way. Each classification category can consist of up to five criteria and as many attributes as you wish.

Account classification structure is as show below picture:

Account classification structure

Criteria				Attributes	Values
SOrg	DChanl	Division	Country	Attribute	Value
3020	Wholesale	High tech	US	Role	Customer
2200	Wholesale			Role	Prospect
2200		Service		Role	Competitor
3120	Wholesale		CA	Rating	Gold
1000	Wholesale		DE	Rating	Silver
1100	Partner			Role	Customer

17) From technical point of view, the SAP CRM product master is a collection or arrangement of which of the following?

a) Classifications
b) Set types
c) Hierarchies
d) All of the above

Answer: b

Explanation:

Attributes help to describe products or individual objects. They are grouped into set types. These set types enable you to perform detailed modelling of products and objects in the system. Set types are the building blocks of the Product master data. Set types are delivered with the SAP CRM system which contains the necessary product information.

Set Types and Attributes

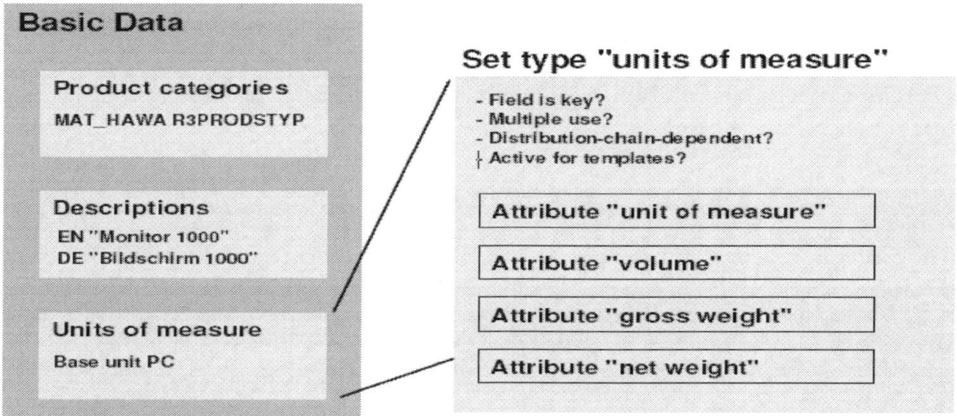

18) Which field/attribute in the SAP CRM business partner record defines which account groups are assigned to a customer master when replicating from SAP CRM to SAP ERP?

a) Account grouping
b) Business partner category
c) Account type
d) Classification

Answer: d

Explanation:

Classification is derived from the role category. In SAP CRM the role categories Sold-to-Party, Ship-to-Party, Bill-to-Party and Payer are assigned to the classification **Customer.** This classification then is assigned to exactly one account group.

Via transaction code PIDE in SAP ERP systems, the mapping of classifications to Account groups and vice versa can be maintained.

Mapping of Classifications and Account Groups

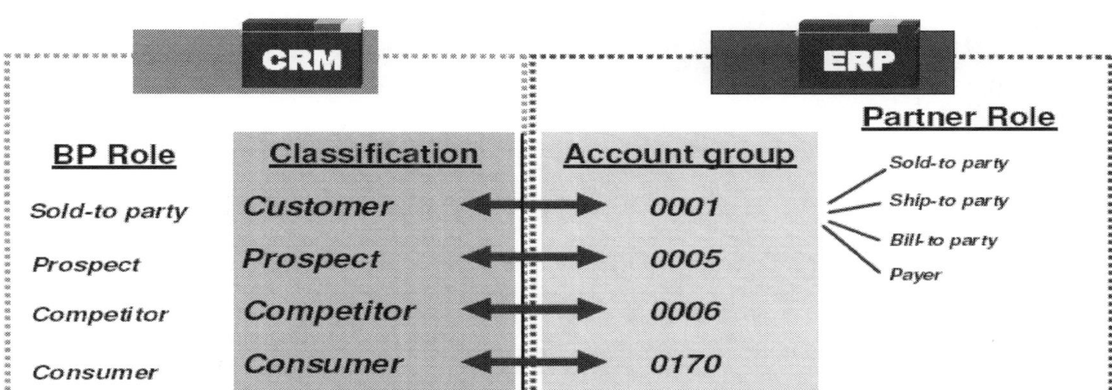

19) **The account hierarchy allows you to group accounts in a multi-level group hierarchy. Which of the following are the two categories of hierarchies? (Choose more than one option)**

a) Contact management
b) Account classification
c) Pricing
d) Statistical

Answer: c, d

Explanation:

You can create account hierarchies in different categories such as the "Pricing" or "Statistics" category. An account can be assigned several hierarchies from different categories. The account hierarchy is sales area-independent, including its different hierarchy levels and nodes.

Hierarchy Categories

Pricing Categories:

- Conditions and price agreements are assigned to hierarchy nodes.
- Conditions and price agreements apply to all accounts that are assigned to the subordinate hierarchy nodes and are dependent on the Customizing settings pricing.

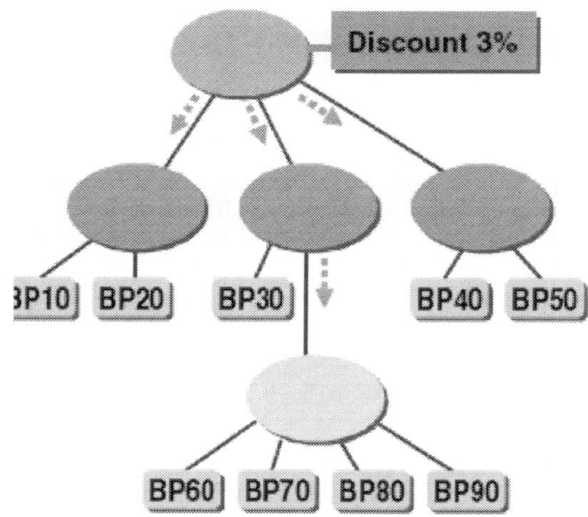

Reporting Structure:

- Business partners are grouped together in a hierarchy for statistical and analytical purposes.

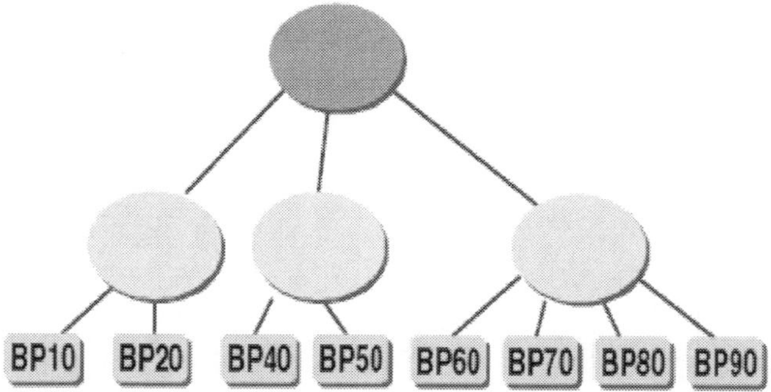

20) With reference to the Org Model in CRM, which of the following statements are correct?

a) Validity periods can be set when creating organizational objects

b) The Org structure in CRM has to be identical to the Org structure in ERP
c) A matrix Org structure can be mapped within CRM
d) All of the above

Answer: a

Explanation:

The organization structure in the CRM system can be different from the structure in the ERP system.

You cannot map a matrix Org structure with the CRM organizational model.

Validity periods can be specified when creating organizational objects and object attributes, and when assigning organizational objects and object characteristics.

For example, a new sales office will open on the first of January next year. In this scenario you can define this sales office by mentioning the validity period and assign it to an organizational model today.

21) Examples of functions of an Organizational unit include: (Choose more than one option)

a) Sales Organisation
b) Postal code
c) Sales group
d) Country
e) Service Organization
f) Transaction type

Answer: a, c, e

Explanation:

The following table explains functions and attributes of an organization Unit:

Functions	General Attributes
Used to define the type of organization unit.	Used to define the responsibilities of an organization unit.
One or more functions can be assigned to an organizational unit.	Several general attributes can be assigned to organizational unit.
Examples:	Examples:
Sales Organization	Country
Sales Office	Division
Sales group	Distribution Channel
Service organization	Postal Code
Marketing organization	Transaction Type

22) Examples of General attributes for an Organizational unit include: (Choose more than one option)

a) Sales Organisation
b) Postal code
c) Sales group
d) Country
e) Service Organization
f) Transaction type

Answer: b, d, f

Explanation:

Below diagram explains it clearly

Functions	General Attributes
Used to define the type of organization unit. One or more functions can be assigned to an organizational unit. Examples: Sales Organization Sales Office Sales group Service organization Marketing organization	Used to define the responsibilities of an organization unit. Several general attributes can be assigned to organizational unit. Examples: Country Division Distribution Channel Postal Code Transaction Type

23) Changes to products are synchronized using an initial load. Choose true or false.

a) True

b) False

Answer: b

Explanation:

Material master data is replicated from the ERP system to the CRM system by the CRM middleware.

An initial download must be made first to download the required materials and to display them as products in SAP CRM.

Subsequent changes and new materials in ERP are then transferred by a delta download.

Download of Material Master Data

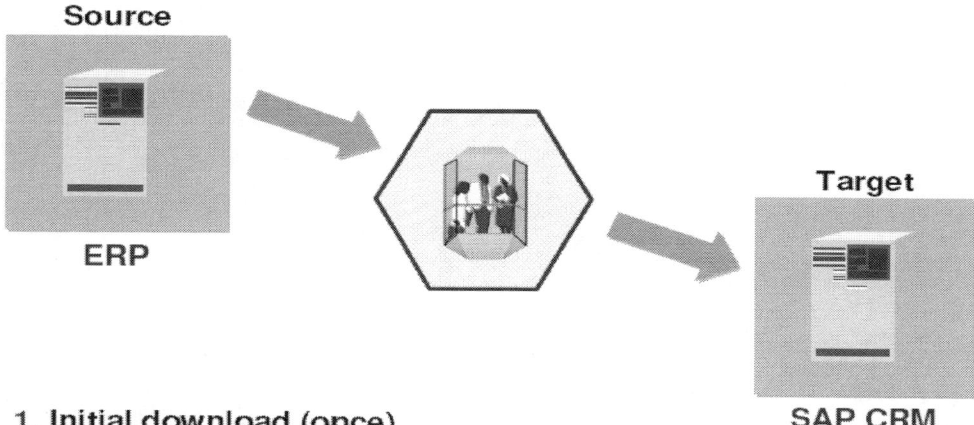

24) Changes to products are synchronized using an initial load. Choose true or false.

a) True
b) False

Answer: b

Explanation:

Material master data is replicated from the ERP system to the CRM system by the CRM middleware.

An initial download must be made first to download the required materials and to display them as products in SAP CRM.

Subsequent changes and new materials in ERP are then transferred by a delta download.

Download of Material Master Data

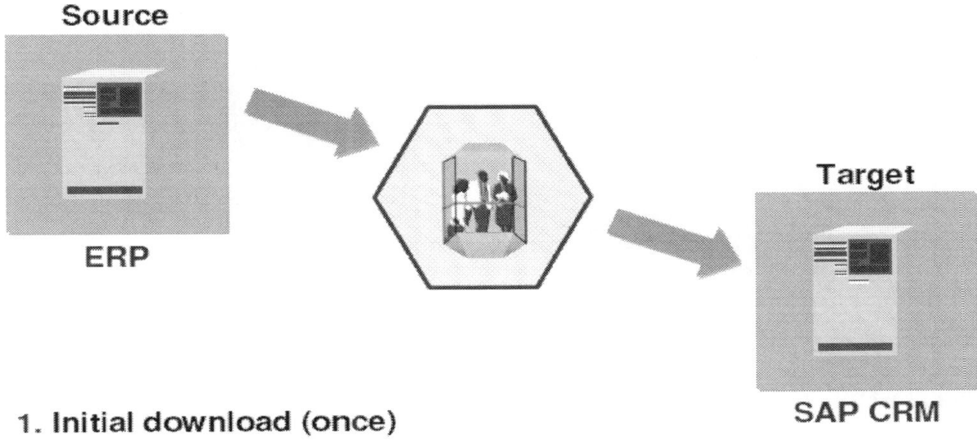

25) You need to enhance the product master in CRM with new fields. Which of the following are the steps required to do this? (Choose more than one option)

a) Assign a set type to a product hierarchy
b) Create a new attribute and a set type
c) Assign a product category to a transaction type
d) Option a & c

Answer: a, b

Explanation:

Products are enhanced by creating new attributes & set types and assigning these to Product categories.

Set types are stored in the system as database tables. Set types enable you to perform detailed modelling of products and objects in the system

26) A task marked as private can only be seen by a sales manager. Choose true or false.

a) True
b) False

Answer: b

Explanation:

A task can be public or private. If a task is private then it can only be seen by the assigned employee.

If the task is Public then all the other employees can also be seen.

27) Which of the following are true? (Choose more than option)

a) A business activity contains information about the interaction with the business partner on a particular date
b) There are four different types of activity: Appointments, interaction logs, e-mails and tasks
c) A task contains information about the activities that one or more employees have to complete by a particular date
d) Items in activities are referred to as interaction log items

Answer: a, b, c

Explanation:

The following are true:

- A business activity contains information about the interaction with the business partner on a particular date
- There are four different types of activity: Appointments, interaction logs, e-mails and tasks
- A task contains information about the activities that one or more employees have to complete by a particular date

Types of Activity

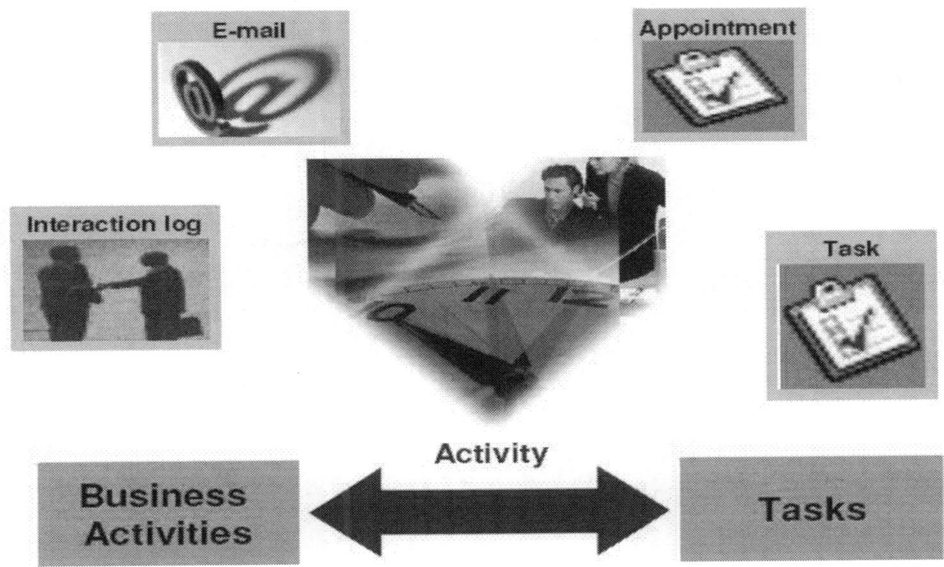

28) Which of the following describes structure of a CRM business transaction?

a) Transaction channels
b) Customizing headers
c) Transaction determination procedure
d) Header, Item, Schedule lines

Answer: d

Explanation:

Standard business transactions like Activities only have header data.

Sales contracts have Header & Item data

Sales orders have Header, Item & Schedule line data

29) The structure of a business transaction depends on:

a) The item it contains
b) The number range
c) The leading business transaction category
d) The leading item category

Answer: c

Explanation:

A business transaction represents a business interaction with a business partner.

The structure of a business transaction depends on the leading business transaction category (for example, Contact, opportunity, sales, service.

General Structure of Transactions

Business Transaction

Business Partners

General data, such as
Description
Priority
Sales cycle
Purchase order number
Pricing procedure
Status
Subject
...

Material 1 Quantity

Material 2 Quantity

Service 1 Quantity

Item-specific data, such as
Pricing relevance
ATP relevance
Confirmation relevance
Resource planning relevance
Billing relevance
...

30) All business transactions have only 2 levels- Header and Item. Choose true or false.

a) True
b) False

Answer: b

Explanation:

Example, Activities have header only and Sales order have a third level- Schedule line. Whereas Opportunity, Lead have both Header & Item levels.

31) Which of the following are factors in determination of item categories?

a) Transaction type
b) Item type
c) Main item type
d) Transaction type usage

Answer: a

Explanation:

Following diagram explains the factors influencing item category determination.

Customizing: Item Category Determination

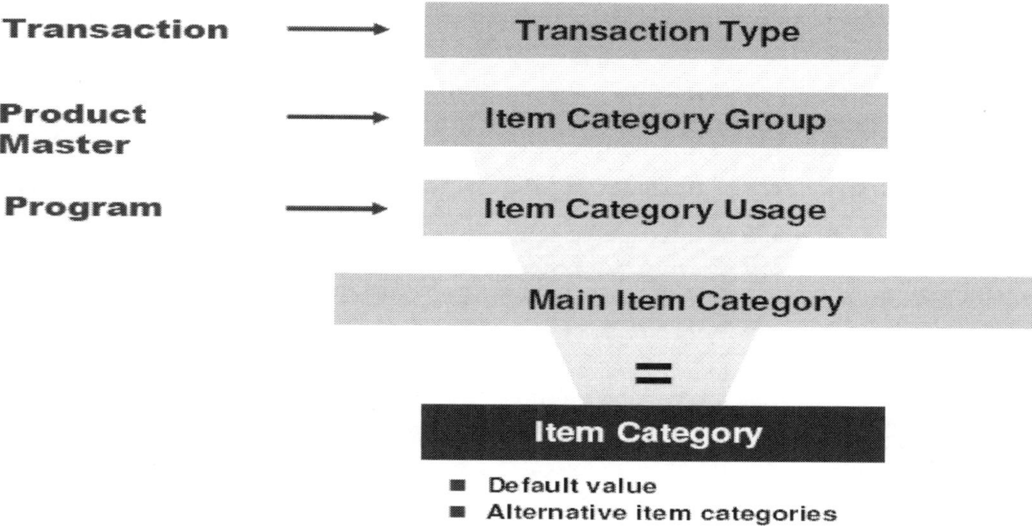

32) Which of the following are true of business transactions? (Choose more than one option)

a) Copied transactions have the same transaction type
b) Follow-up transactions are linked to their preceding documents
c) Copied transactions require copying control settings
d) Header and Item data can be copied to follow-up transactions

Answer: a, b, d

Explanation:

Following table explains the difference between Copy and Follow-up:

Create Follow – Up Transaction	Copy

Data Copied from a business transaction:	Copies current transaction document:
• You can choose the transaction type of the follow-up transaction • Header data is copied. • You can select items • Transaction history is updated Prerequisite: Copy control settings.	• Same transaction type • Header data and item data is copied • Transaction history is not updated; no relationship to predecessor

33) Which of the following statements regarding basic customizing of business transaction is correct? (Choose more than one option)

a) A transaction type contains all relevant item categories
b) An item category can be linked to only one transaction type
c) An item category can contain other item categories
d) A transaction type may have no item category determination

Answer: c, d

Explanation:

A higher level Item category can have predefined allowed lower level item categories. Hence an item category can contain other item categories.

A transaction like an activity or a task has no item level data hence item category determination may not be needed.

34) Within activity transactions which of the following can be used to record and update product related information gathered from customer visits or telephone calls?

a) Actions
b) Activity Journals
c) Product promotion list

d) Texts

Answer: b

Explanation:

Activity journals are used by sales employees during or after an activity, for example, to record all information gathered from a customer visit or telephone call. An activity journal may contain information on products discussed with customer, feedback from the customer, or information on an upcoming event.

Activity journals can contain:

- Products or product categories
- Product-related information such as what products were discussed with the customer, or the number of samples given to the customer.

Activity Journal

Product	Discussed	Number of Samples	Priority
XT-2006	✓	8	High
XT-2007	✓	2	Medium

Notes
Customer is considering ordering XT-2006 in second quarter of 2007.

35) The Sales manager at your company needs a tool that can provide statistics on the number of activities completed by category by department? Which tool would you recommend?

a) Activity Journal
b) Activity Monitor
c) Pipeline Analysis
d) All of the above

Answer: b

Explanation:

The Activity Monitor is a GUI based transaction that allows you to select activities using various criteria. You can adjust the list that is displayed using SAP List Viewer function.

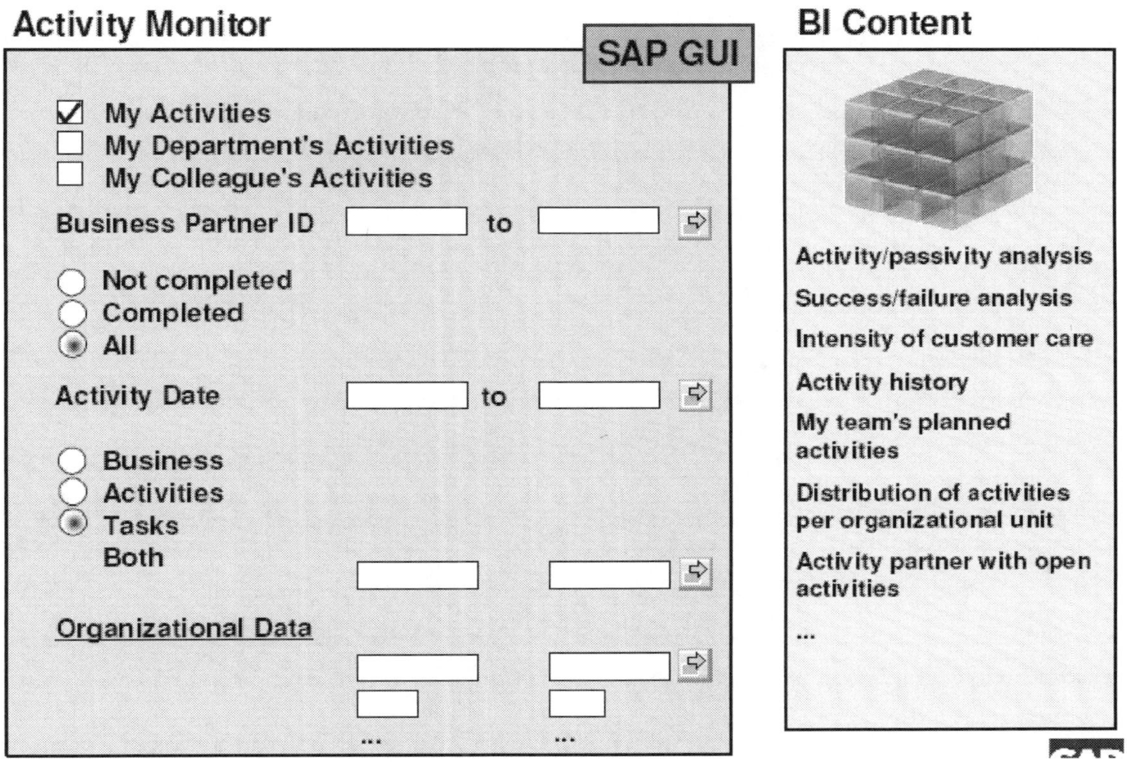

Activity Monitor — SAP GUI

- [x] My Activities
- [ ] My Department's Activities
- [ ] My Colleague's Activities

Business Partner ID ___ to ___

( ) Not completed
( ) Completed
(•) All

Activity Date ___ to ___

( ) Business
( ) Activities
(•) Tasks
Both

Organizational Data

...

BI Content

Activity/passivity analysis
Success/failure analysis
Intensity of customer care
Activity history
My team's planned activities
Distribution of activities per organizational unit
Activity partner with open activities
...

36) **Text data can be maintained in a business transaction at the header or item level. What identifies which texts will be available in a transaction?**

a) Text Profile
b) Text determination procedure
c) Notes assignment profile
d) Text types

Answer: b

Explanation:

The following steps are involved in setting up text determination:

- Define Text Object e.g. CRM_ORDERH
- Define Text Id e.g. Header note, Internal note
- Define Text Determination procedure
- Assign Text determination procedure to transaction type/item category.

37) Which of the following can be assigned to a transaction type? (Choose more than one option)

a) Text profile
b) Date profile
c) Status
d) Incompleteness procedure

Answer: b, d

Explanation:

Text determination procedure can be assigned to a transaction type to determine the texts.

Date profile can be assigned to a transaction type that controls which reference objects, time duration, date types, and date rules can be used in a specific transaction type.

Status profile can be assigned to a transaction type in order to display user statuses in the transaction.

Incompleteness procedure can be assigned to a transaction type. Here you can group fields that you want to check for incompleteness. If you do not enter data in any of these fields in the business transaction, the transaction is considered incomplete.

38) Text determination procedures are designed to govern : (Choose more than one option)

a) Which applications can use it
b) Which text types should be displayed
c) Which text types are mandatory or display only

d) To define the text size
e) How text should be determined

Answer: a, b, c, e

Explanation:

Text determination Procedure:

- Which applications can use the procedure (that is, determine text objects)/
- Which text types should be displayed? (For example, internal note, customer inquiry, report)
- How should texts in the document be processed? (Mandatory or optional, changeable and so on)
- How should the texts be determined? (Access sequence: template object and template text type)

39) CRM uses system status and user status. Choose true or false

a) True
b) False

Answer: a

Explanation:

System statuses: If a status profile (for the user status) is not assigned to a transaction type/item categories, system statuses are displayed in the application (in the transaction).

User statuses: If a status profile (for the user status) is assigned to a transaction type/item categories, user statuses are displayed in the application (in the transaction).

Difference between System Status and Current Status

System Status (SAP Standard)	User Status (Customer Status)
Meaning determined by SAP standard Examples: • Open • In Processing • Error • Complete • Distribution Lock	Can be defined in status profile in any way Examples: • Customer Action • To Release • Released • Rejected • Triggered

40) Which types of conditions do actions use? (Choose more than one option)

a) Start condition
b) Action conditions
c) Access sequence
d) Schedule condition

Answer: a, d

Explanation:

Actions refer to the Post Processing Framework (PPF) Basic components, which can automatically trigger output, follow-up activities or workflows.

Schedule Condition: The schedule condition decides whether an action should be schedule for processing. An action is therefore generated (visible) only if the schedule condition is met.

Start Condition: The start condition is checked before the action is executed. The action is executed only if the start condition is met.

41) Processing times for actions include: (Choose more than one option)

a) Immediately
b) Five minute delay
c) When saving
d) When changing business transaction
e) Selection Report

Answer: a, c, e

Explanation:

The following picture shows the actions included for Processing Time:

Processing Time

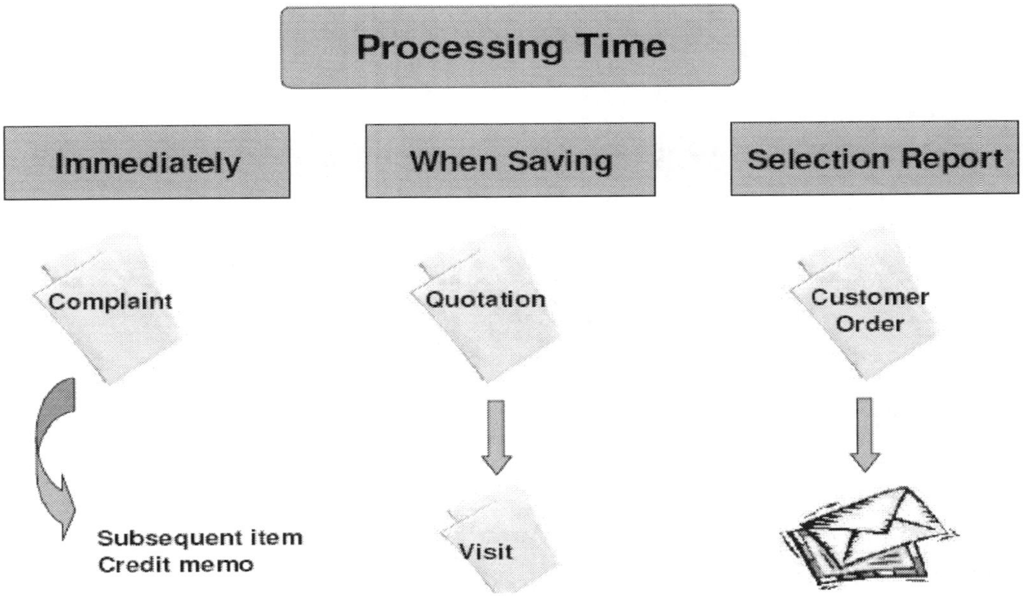

Processing Time
Immediately
When Saving
Selection Report
Complaint
Quotation
Customer Order
Subsequent item Credit memo
Visit

If you select '*Immediately*' as the processing time, the action is started as soon as the start condition is fulfilled.

If you configure the system so that processing starts when '*saving*', the action is started when the transaction is saved.

If you define the processing with the '*selection report*' and the start condition has been fulfilled, the action is started after the execution of a selection report.

42) Processing types for actions include: (Choose more than one option)

a) Smart forms
b) Smart Templates
c) Workflow
d) Methods
e) Web Methods

Answer: a, c, d

Explanation:

SAP Smart forms are used for activities such as printing, e-mailing and faxing documents such as order confirmations.

Actions can create an event to start a workflow.

Methods are Business Add-in (BADI) implementations.

The following picture shows actions included in Processing Types:

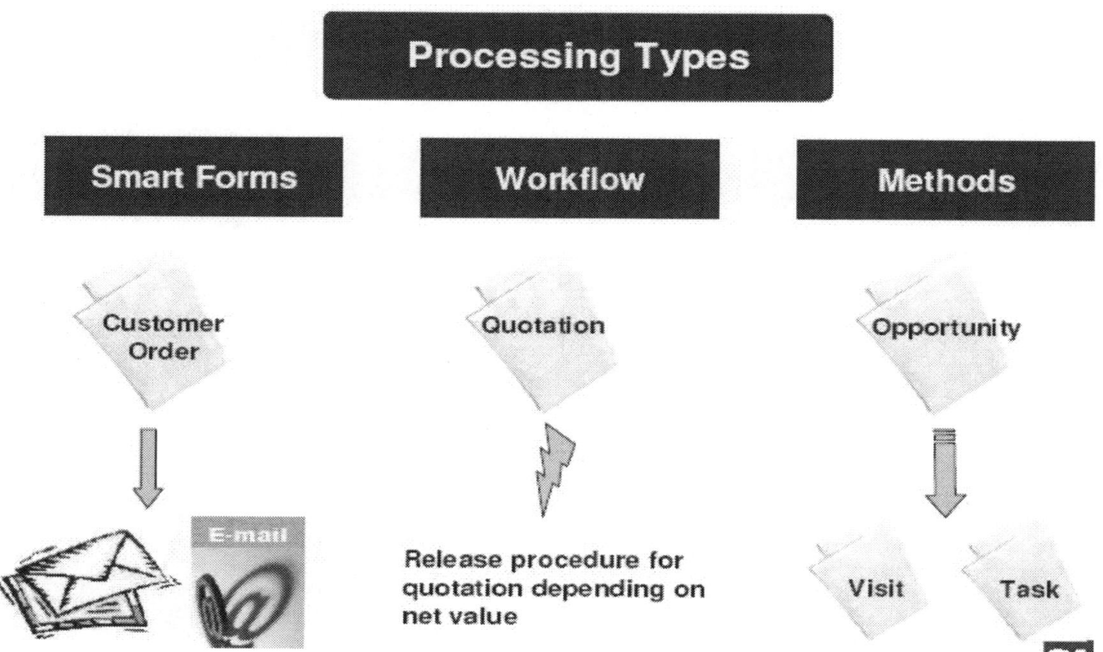

SAP CRM Basic Functions

1) Action profile can only be assigned to transaction types.

a) True
b) False

Answer: b

Explanation:

Action profiles can also be assigned to item categories. An action profile is determined from the corresponding transaction type or item category.

You can assign action profiles directly to a transaction type/item category.

The following picture shows Action Processing Workflow:

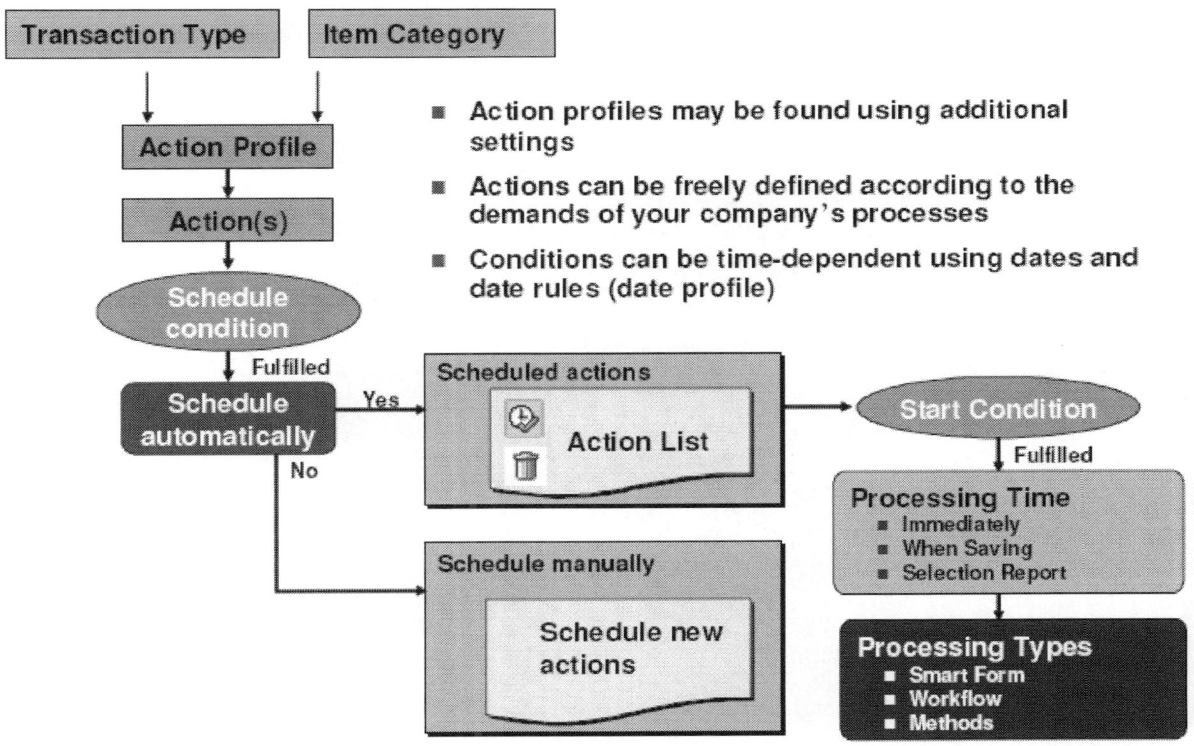

2) IPC is used to handle pricing for which of the following? (Choose more than one option)

a) CRM Web channel
b) CRM Interaction centre
c) Sales order processing in ECC
d) CRM Mobile
e) CRM Analytics

Answer: a, b, d

Explanation:

The Internet Pricing and Configuration (IPC) are used for pricing in SAP CRM scenarios. It is responsible for pricing throughout the entire SAP CRM application.

Pricing information in the internet (CRM Web Channel), CRM Enterprise and mobile clients (such as laptops) is processed by this component.

Below diagram explains about IPC:

Pricing and Tax Determination in SAP CRM

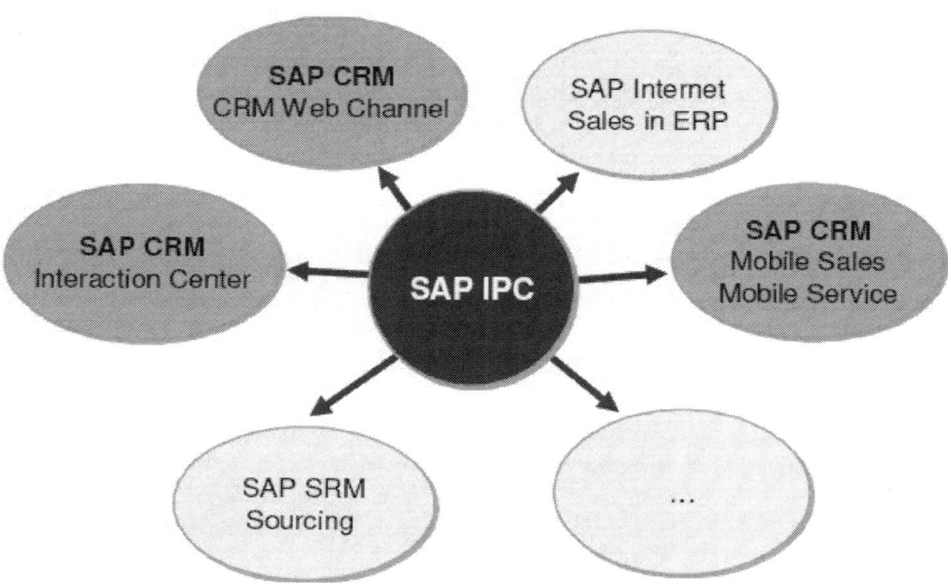

3) Pricing condition records maintained in ECC can be edited in CRM.

a) True
b) False

Answer: b

Explanation:

You set up pricing customizing in the ERP system and maintain the conditions there. Both the customizing and the master data can be transferred from the ERP system to SAP CRM via the middleware .The transferred Customizing and conditions in SAP CRM.

Data is maintained in the SAP ERP system. The SAP ERP system supplies the CRM system with this data and the IPC accesses the CRM database.

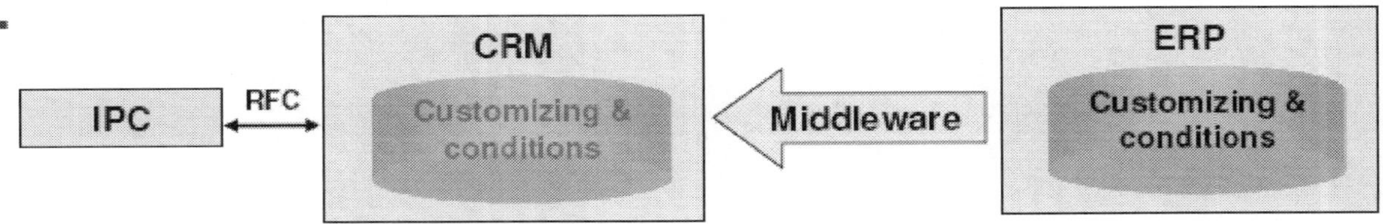

4) What does a Pricing procedure consist of?

a) Transaction type
b) IPC customizing
c) Condition types
d) Document pricing procedure

Answer: c

Explanation:

Pricing procedure consist of valid condition types and their calculation sequence in the transaction.

Pricing procedure defines the following:

- Which subtotals are created and displayed on the pricing screens

- If a condition type is mandatory
- How far the manual processing of pricing is possible

The below picture displays pricing procedure:

Pricing procedure

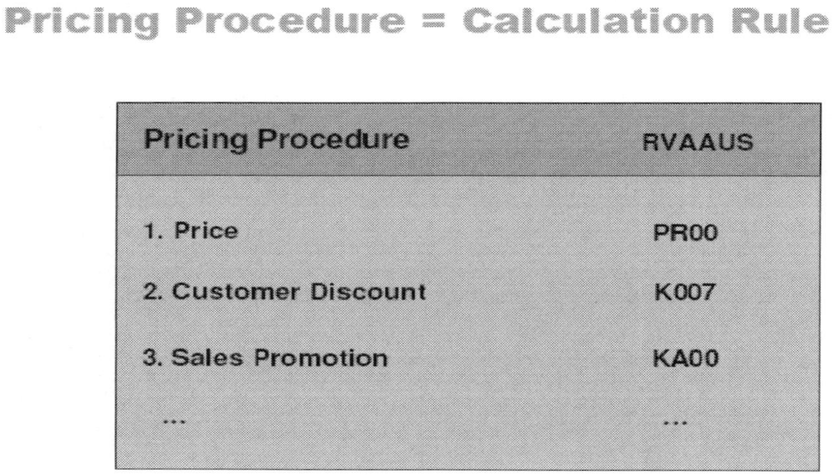

Pricing Procedure = Calculation Rule

Pricing Procedure	RVAAUS
1. Price	PR00
2. Customer Discount	K007
3. Sales Promotion	KA00
...	...

5) **Which of the following are included in determination of Pricing procedure : (Choose more than one option)**

a) Customer pricing procedure
b) Transaction type
c) Distribution Channel
d) Item category
e) Unit of Measure

Answer: a, c

Explanation:

The following elements influence the determination of pricing procedure:

- Sales Organization
- Distribution Channel

- Document pricing procedure
- Customer pricing procedure
- Division(optional)

The following picture displays determination of pricing procedure:

Determination of Pricing Procedure

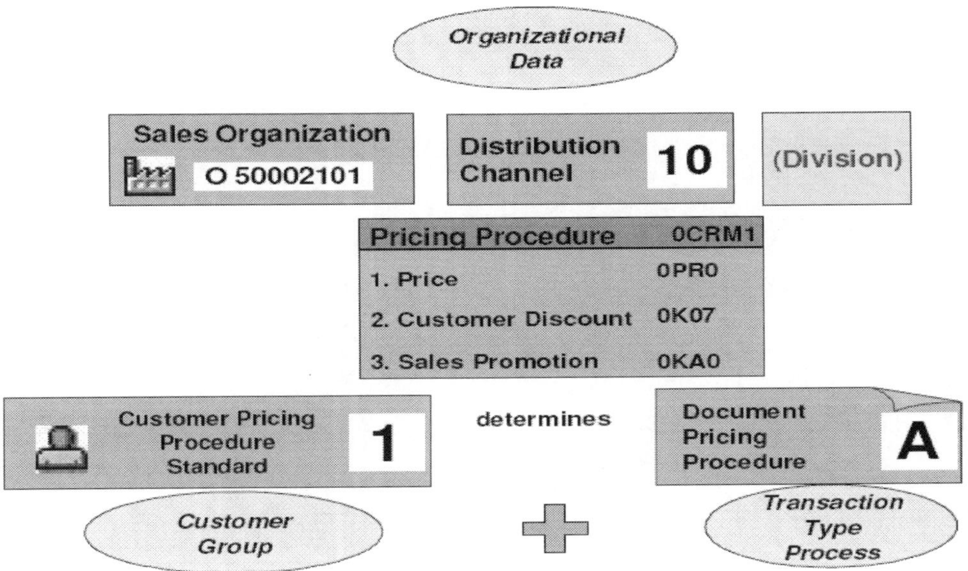

6) What customizing settings are required for condition technique in pricing? (Choose more than one option)

a) Assignment of condition types to pricing procedure
b) Assignment of access sequence to condition types
c) Assignment of condition records to access sequence
d) Assignment of pricing procedure to transaction type

Answer: a, b, d

Explanation:

The below diagram explains about the customizing settings required for condition technique:

Condition Technique

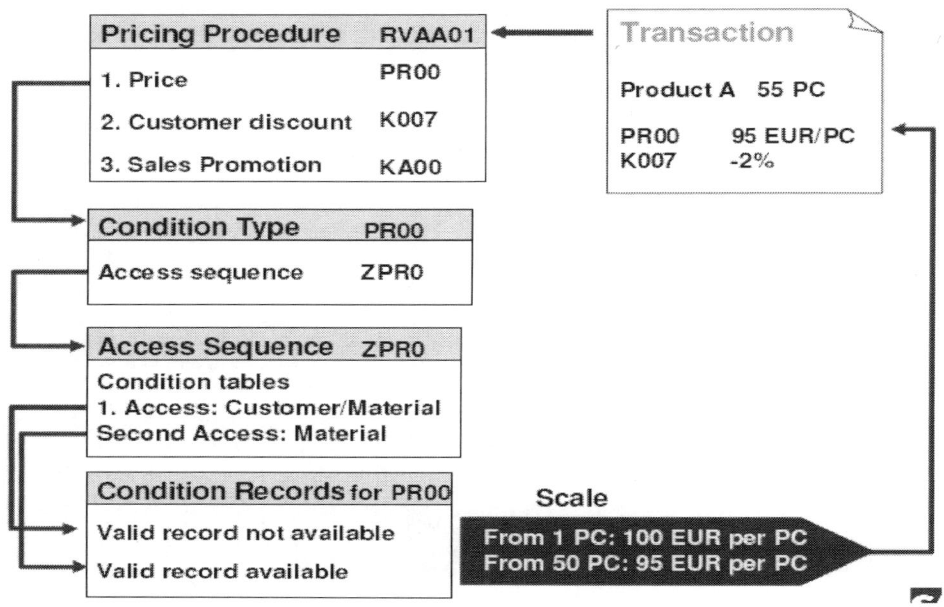

7) How many tables are required for a pricing access sequence

a) Two
b) At least two
c) At least one
d) None

Answer: c

Explanation:

An access sequence is a search strategy that the system uses to search for a valid data in a specific condition type.

It comprises of one or more accesses that are each defined by specifying a condition table and hence pricing access sequence requires at least one table.

Access Sequence

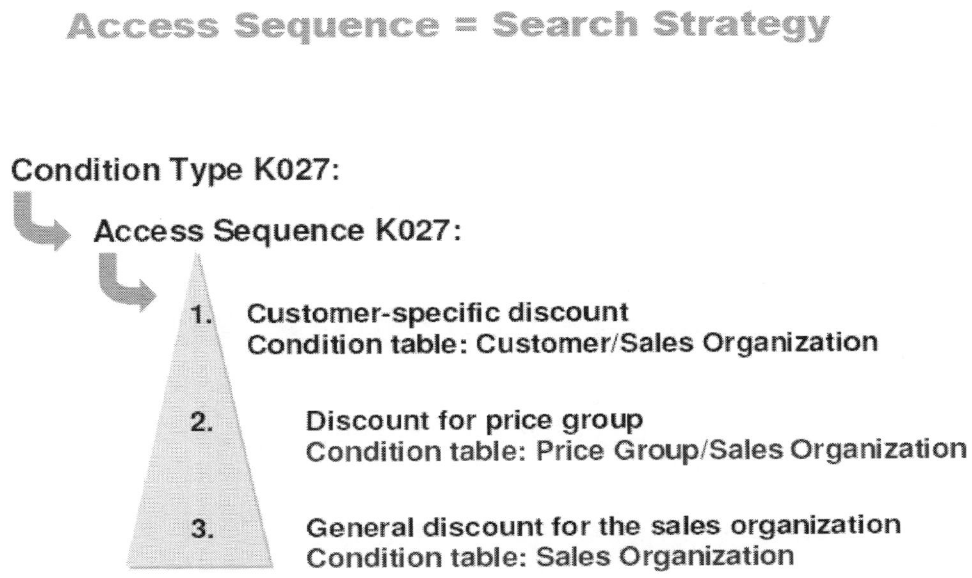

Access Sequence = Search Strategy

Condition Type K027:

Access Sequence K027:

1. Customer-specific discount
Condition table: Customer/Sales Organization

2. Discount for price group
Condition table: Price Group/Sales Organization

3. General discount for the sales organization
Condition table: Sales Organization

8) Which of the following are true of pricing? (Choose more than one option)

a) Validity dates are required in condition records
b) The TTE can be called through the use of condition type 0TTE or 1TTE
c) Scales are only available in one dimension

Answer: a, b

Explanation:

- Data about conditions is stored in condition records.
- You can limit a pricing agreement to a specific period. To do this, specify **Validity period**. This can be useful when you want to have different price lists for different years or have discounts valid only for the duration of a special offer.

Special offer discount:

Level at which the condition is defined

Sales organization	1000
Distribution channel:	01
Customer:	C1
Material:	M1

1st Period March 01 to April 30		2nd Period May 01 to May 30	
$ 1000	- 1 %	$ 1000	- 2 %
$ 2000	- 2 %	$ 2000	- 3 %
$ 3000	- 3 %	$ 3000	- 4 %

9) Condition maintenance can be started from which of the following objects? (Choose more than one option.)

a) Opportunity
b) Business partners
c) Campaigns
d) Billing
e) Contracts

Answer: b, c, e

Explanation:

The objects from which condition maintenance can be started are:

- Business Partners
- Business Partner hierarchies
- Products

- Contracts (Price agreements)
- Campaigns (discounts)

You can also maintain conditions in general condition maintenance.

10) Which of the following modules of SAP integrate with CRM billing? (Choose more than one option)

a) Logistic Execution
b) Plant Maintenance
c) Financial accounting
d) Controlling
e) CRM Sales

Answer: a, c, d, e

Explanation:

Logistic Execution, CRM Sales, Financial accounting, Controlling are integrated with CRM Billing.

The following picture depicts the same:

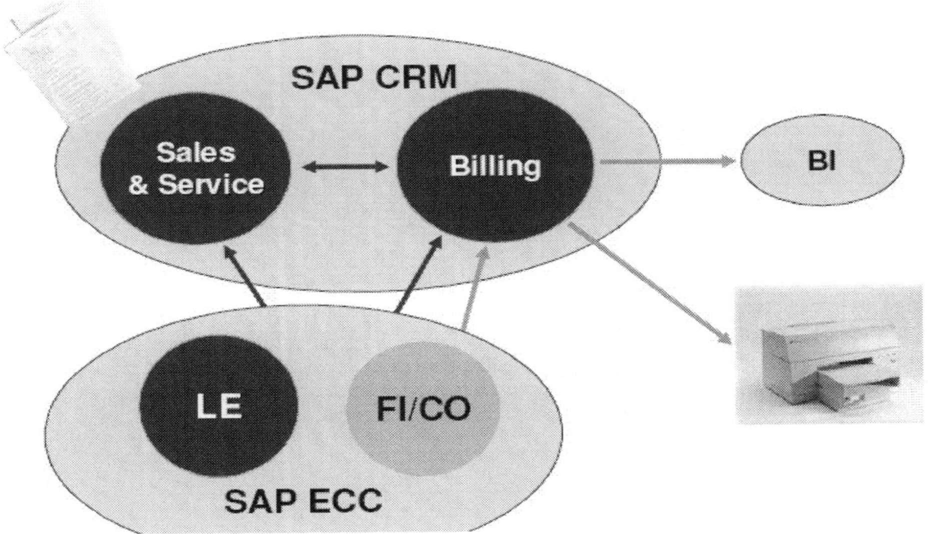

11) Billing relevance is controlled by :

a) Sales transaction type
b) Sales item category
c) Pricing procedure
d) All of the above

Answer: b

Explanation:

When you save a business transaction in which at least one item is relevant to billing, the system automatically transfers the data from this billing request item to the billing due list in CRM billing.

CRM billing uses the data from Customizing to determine the item category in CRM billing for the transferred data record. When the system cannot determine an item category the system has to reject the transferred data record because billing is not possible without the item categories. Hence billing relevance is controlled by Item category.

12) Which of the following billing plans are available in SAP CRM Billing? (Choose more than one option)

a) Collective billing
b) Periodic billing
c) Milestone billing
d) Partial billing

Answer: b, c

Explanation:

The billing plan specifies when a certain amount is involved.

Service contracts and leasing scenarios in particular use billing plans. Below diagram explains about the billing plans available in SAP CRM:

Billing plan procedure + Transaction type/item category ⇒ Billing plan type

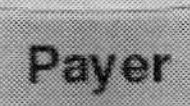

Periodic billing
(for example, contracts)

January — EUR 740.00

February — EUR 740.00

March — EUR 740.00

Milestone billing
(for example, projects)

January — 20% = EUR 100.00

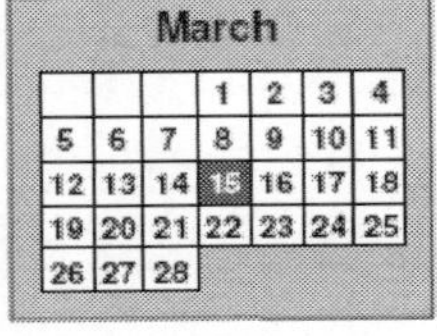

40% = EUR 200.00

May — 40% = EUR 200.00

13) Which of the following steps are parts of CRM billing? (Choose more than one option)

a) Input processing
b) Order integration
c) Billing
d) Output processing

Answer: a, c, d

Explanation:

The billing process consists of three steps:

- Input Processing
- Billing
- Output Processing.

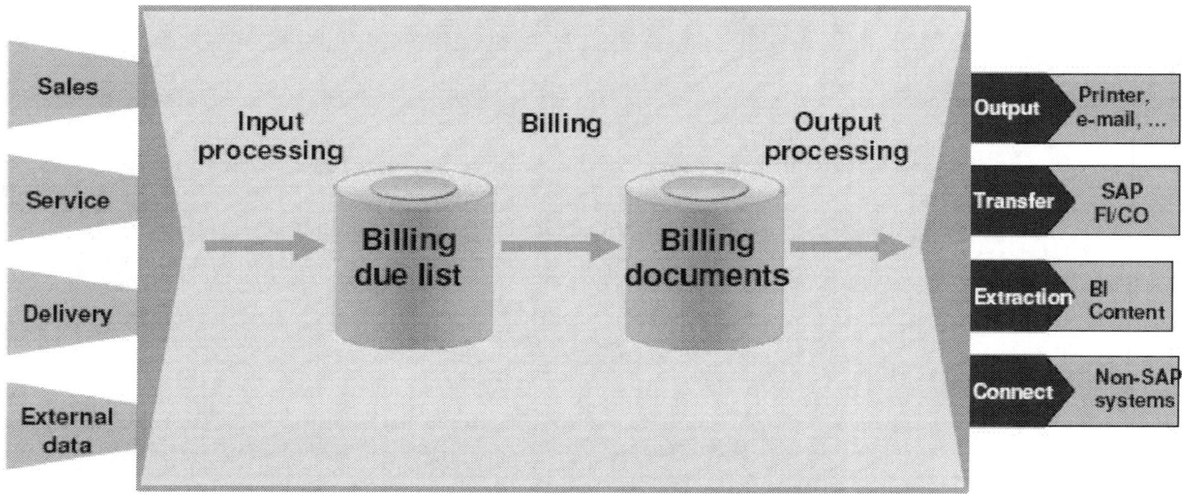

During **Input processing,** CRM billing take over billing-relevant items from different business transactions and saves them as billing due list items.

During **Billing,** the system groups related billing due list items from different business transactions into joint billing document .The billing due list can process due list items as part of an individual billing or as part of collective billing.

14) Items that need to be billed are included in a report called as :

a) Invoice list
b) Billing report
c) Billing due list
d) Billing item list

Answer: c

Explanation:

During input processing, CRM billing takes over billing-relevant items from different business transactions and saves them as billing due list items.

15) Billing documents can be cancelled. Choose true or false.

a) True
b) False

Answer: a

Explanation:

As long as the invoices have not been transferred to accounting, you can make certain changes to the invoices.

You can cancel individual billing documents and also execute collective cancellations. The system transfers cancellation information to financial accounting automatically.

16) Which of the following statements regarding Billing Unit are correct?

a) A billing unit is the CRM business partner that has the role “Billing Unit”
b) Exactly one sales organization can be assigned to a billing unit
c) Billing units have to be defined in the billing unit customizing table
d) Billing units are defined in the Organization structure

Answer: a

Explanation:

- The **billing unit (BU)** is a CRM business partner that has the role Billing Unit. For more information see the IMG documentation:

  SAP Implementation Guide → Customer Relationship Management → Billing → Define Billing Organization Unit.

- The billing unit can be defined separately and independently of the sales or service organization.
- You can assign more than one sales organization to a billing unit (cross-sales organization billing)
- Billing units are assigned uniquely to company codes.

Billing-specific assignments of Organizational units

SAP Reference IMG
Customer Relationship Management
Master Data
Organizational Management
Cross-System Assignments ...

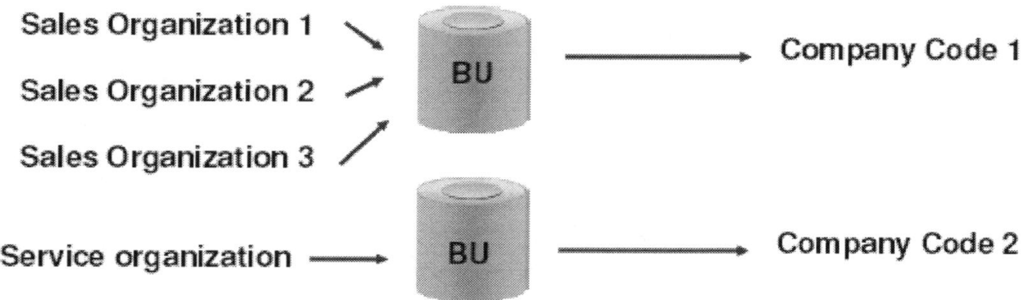

SAP CRM Technology & Integration

1) **Identify some of the SAP solutions provided under the SAP Business Suite. (Choose more than one option)**

   a) SAP ERP (Enterprise Resource Planning)

   b) SAP CRM (Customer Relationship Management)

   c) SAP SCM (Supply Chain Management)

   d) SAP SRM (Supplier Relationship Management)

Answer: a, b, c & d.

Explanation:

The SAP Business Suite consists of the following SAP Solutions:

- SAP ERP (Enterprise Resource Planning)
- SAP CRM (Customer Relationship Management)
- SAP SCM (Supply Chain Management)
- SAP PLM (Product Life Cycle Management)
- SAP SRM (Supplier Relationship Management)

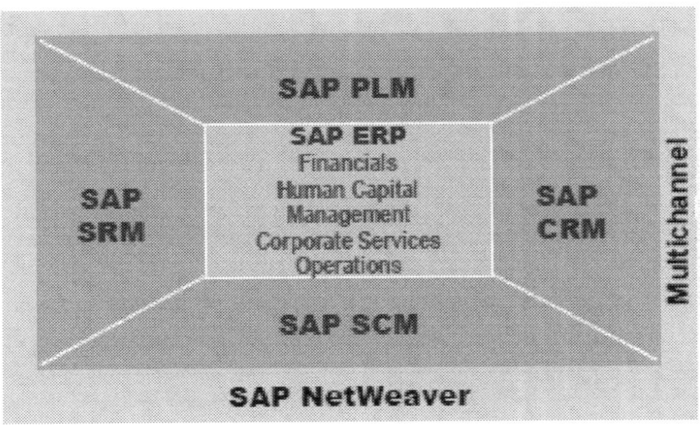

2) Which SAP system used as a data warehouse solution with comprehensive statistical analysis functions?

a) The SAP ERP

b) The SAP BI

c) The SAP SCM

d) The SAP XI

Answer: b.

Explanation:

The SAP CRM solution offers you the following, fully-integrated connections:

- The SAP CRM system as a central CRM server with corresponding application components
- The SAP ERP system as a back-end system with tried and true ERP functions
- The SAP BI system as a data warehouse solution with comprehensive statistical and analysis functions
- The SAP SCM system as a data warehouse solution with comprehensive statistical and analysis functions
- The SAP NetWeaver Portal as a tool that provides you with integrated access to all systems

3) Identify the application components that are supported in SAP CRM? (Choose more than one option)

a) Interaction center

b) Web Channel (Internet)

c) Mobile clients

d) None of the above

Answer: a, b & c

Explanation:

Interaction center: Using integrated Interaction Center Solutions, clients can contact sales or service representatives by telephone, fax or email.
Web Channel (Internet): Internet users may configure and order products or services using SAP CRM Internet components.
Mobile Clients/Handhelds: Mobile sales representatives and service engineers can access the SAP CRM system from their laptops or other mobile devices to exchange up-to-date information with central CRM server.

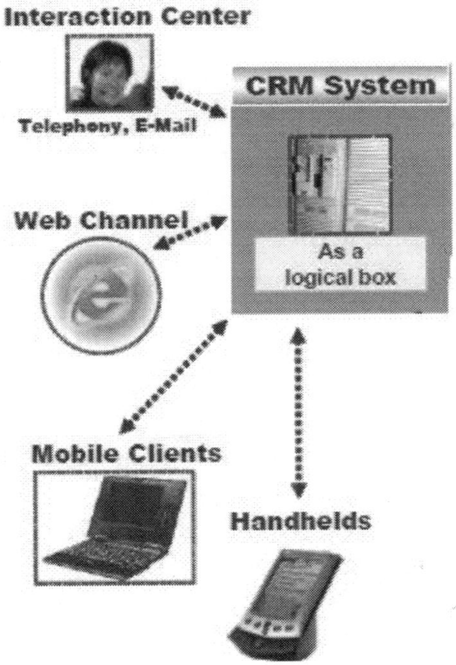

4) Which adapter is used in SAP CRM to establish communication with SAP ERP system?

a) BW Adapter

b) R/3 Adapter

c) External Adapter

d) No Adapter is required

Answer: b.

Explanation:

Data is exchanged between the CRM system and a connected ERP system using the CRM middleware.

A plug- in is installed in the ERP system acts as a counterpart to the R/3 adapter in the SAP ERP system. It supports data communication between these two systems.

R/3 adapter is used within the SAP CRM which provides the communication between SAP CRM and SAP ERP system.

You can see the below screen shot for your reference:

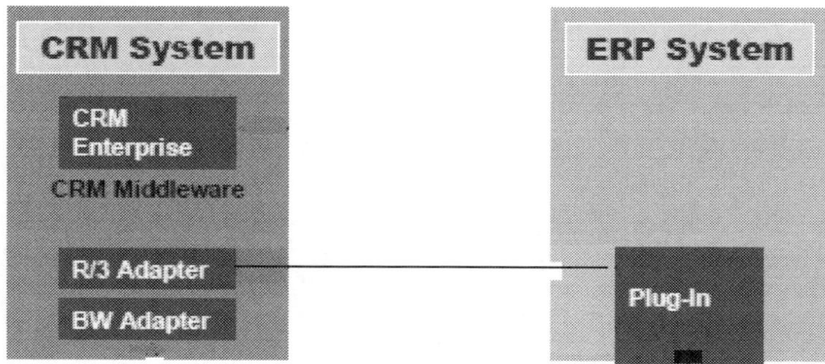

5) Which component provides configuration and pricing data for Web Applications?

a) Internet Communication Frame work

b) Index server and search Engine

c) Internet Pricing and Configurator

d) Web Channels

Answer: c.

Explanation:

Internet Pricing and Configurator (IPC) is used to configure and price products in a Web environment, using master data downloaded from your SAP R/3 System or directly transferred from a Customer Relationship Management (CRM) system.

The Internet Pricing and Configurator combines the functions of the Sales Configuration Engine (SCE) and the Sales Pricing Engine (SPE) with a standardized Web interface, which can be easily adapted to match your corporate image. Customers can access your Web site, view and select product options, see how much their choice costs, and trigger a sales order. You can then upload the order information to your R/3 System.

6) The SAP CRM Interaction center supports the communication channel "Voice over Internet Protocol" (VoIP).

a) True

b) False

Answer: a

Explanation:

Voice over Internet protocol (VoIP) is a collection of communication protocols over Internet Protocol (IP) networks such as the Internet.

The SAP CRM Interaction center supports communication channel Voice over Internet Protocol along with other communication channels such as Telephone, Email and Fax.

7) Which system can be used to connect the communication channels Telephone and E-mail with SAP CRM Interaction center?

a) SAP BCM

b) SAP CRM

c) SAP BI

d) SAP XI

Answer: a.

Explanation:

SAP Business Communications Management (SAP BCM) provides an advanced, all-IP communication solution for multichannel contact centers and contact-intensive, multisite organizations. It replaces traditional communications systems hardware with a software-based IP telephony solution that can help make your staff's interactions with customers and partners more effective.

Intelligent routing ensures that customers reach the right people within your organization – people with the skills to best address the customers' needs. Plus, unified queuing, prioritizing, and routing of all contacts, no matter their format – telephone, e-mail, fax, voicemail, text messaging, and the Web – ensures that your users have a smooth, consistent experience

SAP BCM uses the Online Interaction Interface (OII) package to communicate with external applications. If not already present you therefore need to add this module to the BCM System by installing the Integration Services component. The Integration package contains a number of web services that are deployed to the IIS web server. The integration Services package should therefore be added to the Virtual Unit that runs the web server.

8) Which component is used to connect the mobile clients to the SAP CRM server?

a) Ports manager

b) Solution Manager

c) Communication Station

d) Service Manager

Answer: c

Explanation:

Mobile clients usually connect to the CRM server for data exchange.

The communication station is used connect the mobile clients to the CRM server.

Communication station sits between your mobile client and CRM server and acts as a channel of regulating the data exchange on your mobile client. Communication station is basically a system which hosts a SAP CRM Transfer Service (a COM+ application).

You can see the below screen shot for your clear understanding of the connections between CRM server and Mobile clients:

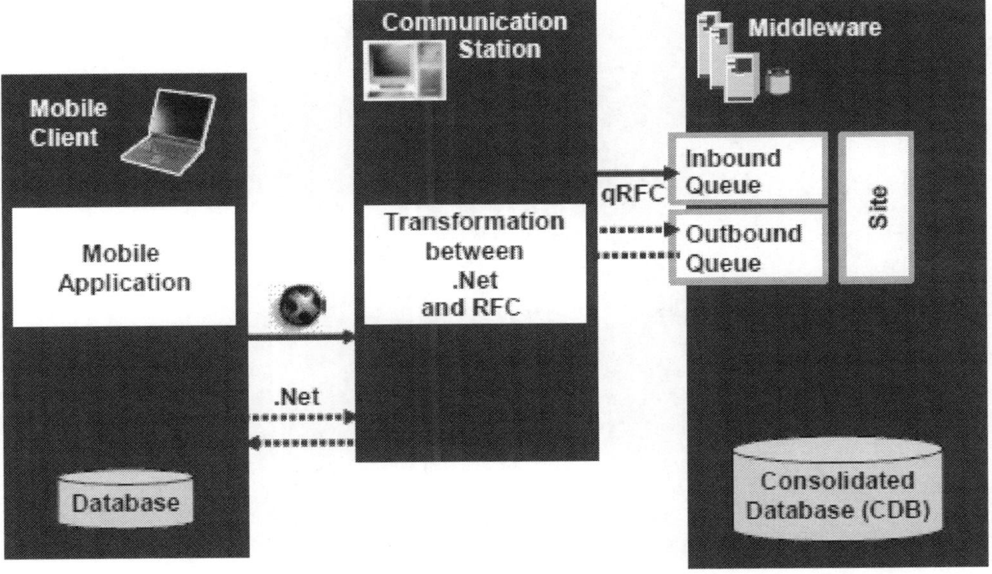

9) Which User Interface is the current evolution in the context of SAP CRM?

a) SAP GUI

b) IC Web Client

c) PCUI

d) CRM Web Client

Answer: d

Explanation:

The user friendly interface is the key to success the SAP CRM implementation. The CRM Web Client User Interface fulfils all requirements in a perfect way and is the result of the UI evolution based on customer.

The CRM Web Client UI is based on Business Server Page Technology.

You can see the evolution of User Interfaces in the below diagram:

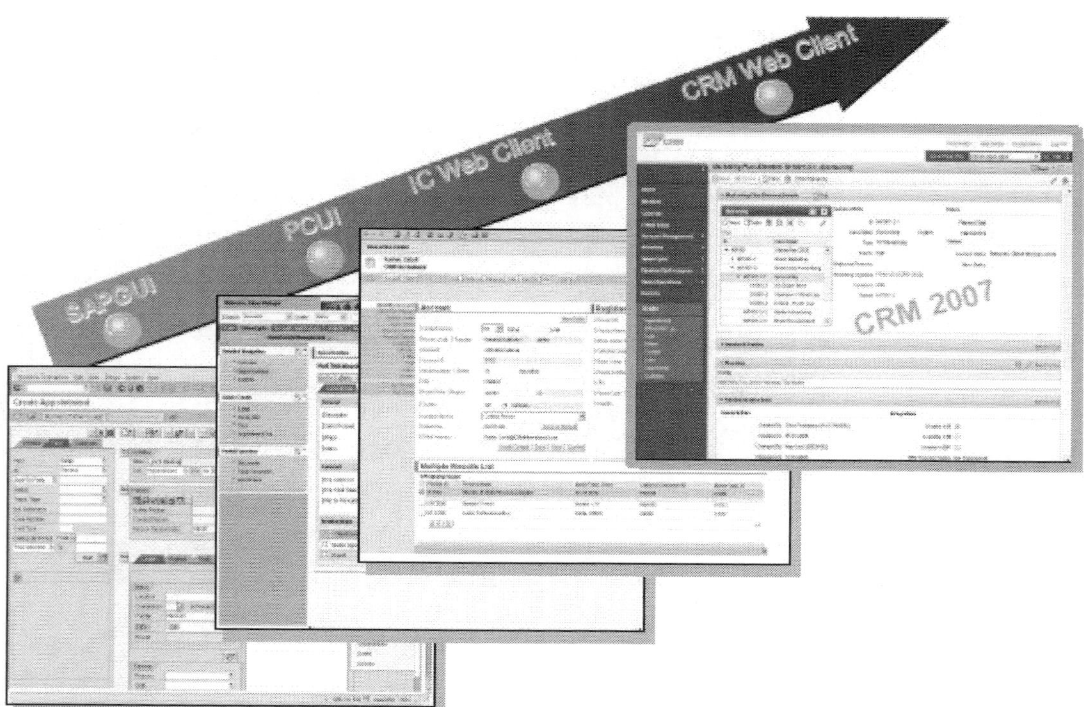

10) What are the main elements of User Interface? (Choose more than one option)

a) Work Area Title

b) Work Area tool bar

c) Header Area

d) Assignment Blocks

Answer: a, b, c & d.

Explanation:

The main elements of User Interface are:

- Work Area Title
- Work Area Tool bar
- Header Area
- Assignment Blocks

You can see the overview page below:

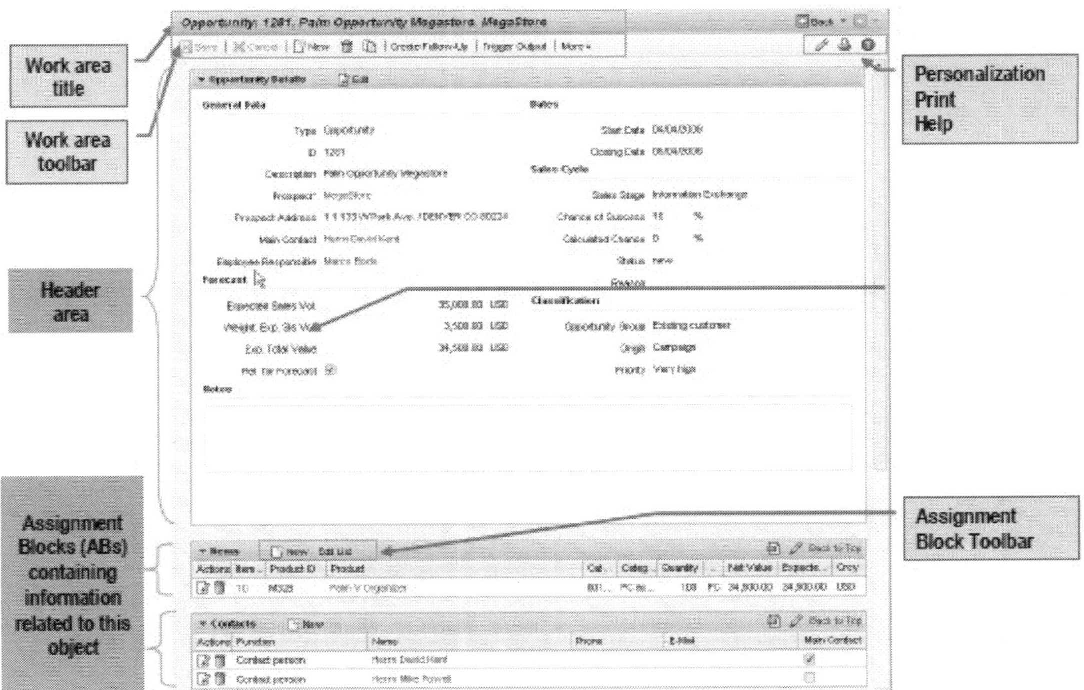

11) What is the general method used for customer segmentation?

a) Scoring

b) Clustering

c) Decision Trees

d) All the above

Answer: b.

Explanation:

During Customer Segmentation with Cluster Analysis, the system determines homogeneous customer segments from a large amount of customer data. The system uses the data mining method clustering to group together into customer segments all customers sharing the same profile, such as all customers under a given age with a low income and less than two children. In this process, the system determines segmentation criteria as well as which customers are to be assigned to which segment.

Process Steps in Clustering Method:

- SAP CRM and SAP R/3 provide master and transaction data concerning your customers
- SAP BW updates the data in the customer knowledge base.
- You determine the dimensions relevant for clustering and their importance.
- SAP BW determines the customer segments.
- You analyze the customer segments determined.
- You update the master data in the customer knowledge base.
- You perform target group creation and campaign management.

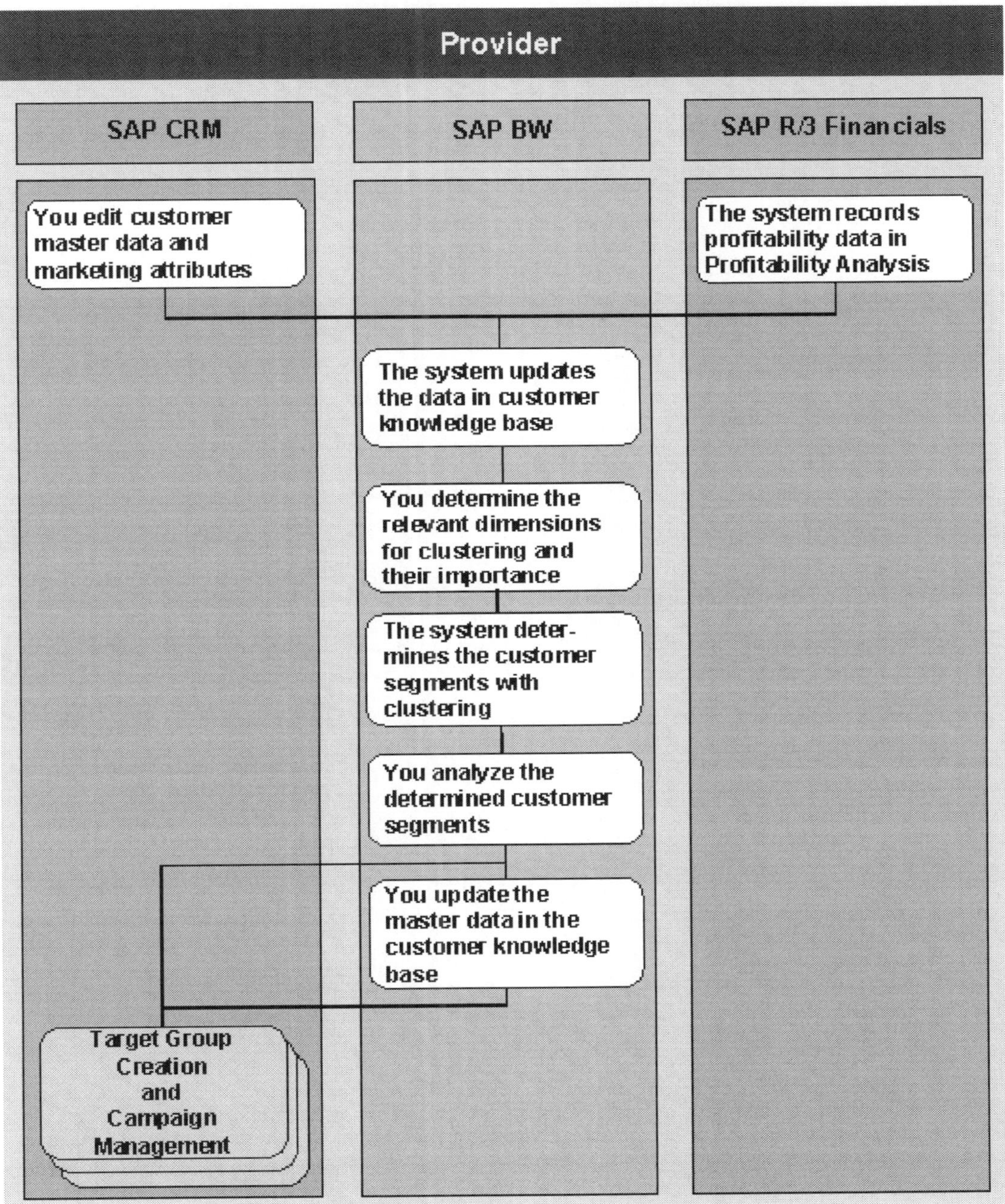

Scoring is used to bring them together different aspect of an overall evaluation.

Decision Trees is used to determine the most important dimensions from a larger amount of possible dimensions.

SAP CRM Business Scenarios

1) **You are a consultant responsible for configuring the marketing module in an implementation. You hold a workshop with the client and the following statements are made at the workshop. Which of these statements are true?**

    a) Campaigns help define strategic goals, whereas marketing plans focus on the execution

    b) Campaigns can be structured hierarchically under a Marketing Plan, however this is optional

    c) It is mandatory to assign the Target groups to marketing plan

    d) A target group can be assigned to multiple profile sets or profile

Answer: b.

Explanation:

Marketing Plans are defined at startegic level. It is used to define budgets, costing in marketing department. You can use any number of marketing plan elements to structure a marketing a plan in the form of a hierarchy.

Campiagns are defined at operating level. It is used to serve the marketing plans and execution. It is used to define product promotions, telemarketing..etc. You can assign one or more campiagns to each marketing plan. It is also possible to create a campaign without assignment to a marketing plan.

A profile is a finite list of characterstics and their values that make up the "profile" of a business partner. A profile set is a type of folder for profiles, target groups and sub groups. A profile has to be assigned to a profile set.

A target group is a finite list of business partners that match a corresponding profile / profile sets. A target group must be assigned to a profile or profile set.

2) Your client wants to start a new campaign to introduce a new product. You are a consultant required to create a new target group based on the attributes like hobbies, region, & Sales Volume. What are the data sources would you consider for segmentation? (Choose more than one option)

a) Info Sets consisting of your own ABAP queries

b) Marketing attribute from the business partner master data

c) Business Intelligence Info cubes

d) SAP SRM elements

Answer: a, b & c

Explanation:

There are three data sources available for target group selection in SAP CRM Marketing. They are:

- SAP BW Reports and Info Cubes
- Info sets consisting of your own ABAP Queries
- Marketing attributes from the business partner master data

The SAP BW Reports and Info Cubes allow you to select a business partner for a target group using master data, profiles or transaction data.

The Info sets from your own ABAP queries evaluate general data from the business partner master record and can be used to select target groups according to address.

You can enter marketing characteristics directly in the business partner master record. Characteristics are then grouped together, creating characteristic groups. You can edit and use them to select a target group.

You can identify the source for segmentation of target groups in the below diagram:

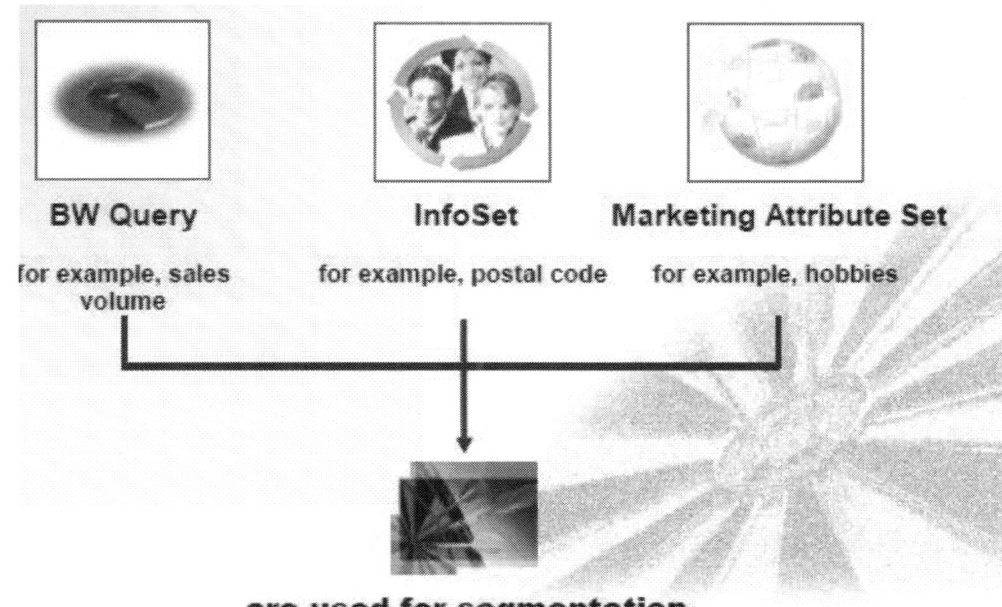

3) **Your client wants to tailor the sales methodology within Opportunity management. Which of the following are Key elements do you consider to optimize the sales process by sales methodology? (Choose more than one option)**

   a) Buying Center

   b) Case Management

   c) Sales assistant

   d) Opportunity assessment

Answer: a, c & d.

Explanation:

A structured sales methodology enables you to manage your sales projects optimally, and thus to increase the effectiveness of the sales process.

Opportunity Management allows you to construct a sales methodology tailored to suit your sales processes. Your sales employees are coached through the steps of an ideal sales process – from identifying the lead to closing the sale.

Sales methodology is incorporated in the following elements within Opportunity Management:

- Sales Assistant

  The sales assistant leads sales employees through a structured sales process, and supports him in planning his sales activities, without restricting his freedom. The sales assistant provides the sales employee with a checklist of recommended activities and tasks that he should execute during this phase. This feature is also available in CRM Mobile.

- Project goals

  You can also store project goals here within the framework of sales methodology. In order to clearly establish how the customer could benefit from your solution, and to position your product strategically, it is important that you really understand customers' requirements and expected results. It clearly defines the short and long-term objectives you hope to achieve. Both your customers' goals and your own goals can be recorded in predefined templates under Notes, and are accessible to all employees involved in the sales process.

- Buying center

  It identifies those persons involved in the buying process, and determines their degree of influence. It Display the relationship network of those persons involved in the sales process, and enter key attributes for each individual, for example, their opinion of your solution and personal value proposition

- Competitor analysis

  You can display competitors and their products at both header and item level. You can create master data for competitors, and create texts for each competitor. Predefined templates are available to help you record this information.

- Opportunity assessment

  You can assign several questionnaires to an opportunity that can be found according to different criteria. You make settings for determination and criteria for determination in Customizing. You can use questionnaires in opportunities, for example, for project qualification, or to analyze won or lost opportunities.

- Opportunity plan

  The opportunity plan combines all the key information about a sales opportunity. It provides you with an extensive overview of the current status of the project, and you can use it as a basis for presentations or discussions during internal project meetings.

4) Your client wants to provide the services and follow-up documents at regular intervals with Service Contract to the customers. Which documents are the enhancements of service contract that provides the follow-up documents at regular intervals?

a) Service Orders

b) Service Plans

c) Service level agreements

d) None of the above

Answer: b.

Explanation:

A service plan is a functional enhancement to the service contract. It is created at the item level of service contract to plan and organize periodic services that should be provided regularly at certain intervals.

In the service plan, services and follow up transactions that are to be carried out regularly are entered, and service intervals and planned dates are calculated and monitored.

The service plan creates maintenance call objects such as a service order or a quotation.

5) You are a consultant configuring the business flow process of the Quotation and Sales Order, Which of the following business process works only in quotation but not in sales order?

a) Availability check

b) Automatic Partner determination

c) Organizational data determination

d) Sales Probability

Answer: d.

Explanation:

You can assign an order probability to a quotation item. It flags the probability that an order will be placed, and is used when calculating the expected total net value in dynamically cumulated document data. Sources for sales probability are:

- The general sales probability of a quotation item defined in Customizing for the item category
- The success rate of a product
- Manual entries in the quotation

Availability check, Partner Determination and Organizational data determination are performed in both Quotation and Sales Order processing.

6) Your client already uses the SAP ERP system and wants to implement SAP CRM. During the implementation of SAP CRM Sales, the following statements have been made. Which of the following are true? (Choose more than one option)

a) Sales Orders can be created with reference to an opportunity.

b) Sales Orders can be transferred to ERP only if they have processed completely without any errors.

c) Billing of Sales Orders must be done in CRM.

d) Sales Orders can be delivered in CRM

Answer: a & b

Explanation:

Sales Orders can be created with reference to an opportunity. Or else a Quotation can be created with reference to an opportunity and sales order is created with reference to quotation. Both cases are possible in the CRM.

Sales orders can be transferred to the ERP system only if they have been processed completely and without errors. If the Sales order contains any errors or incomplete, you cannot transfer it to the ERP system.

Delivery of sales order happens only at SAP ERP. The Transportation and Delivery happens in CRM. Billing of sales order can be done at both systems SAP CRM or SAP ERP.

You can see the process in the below diagram:

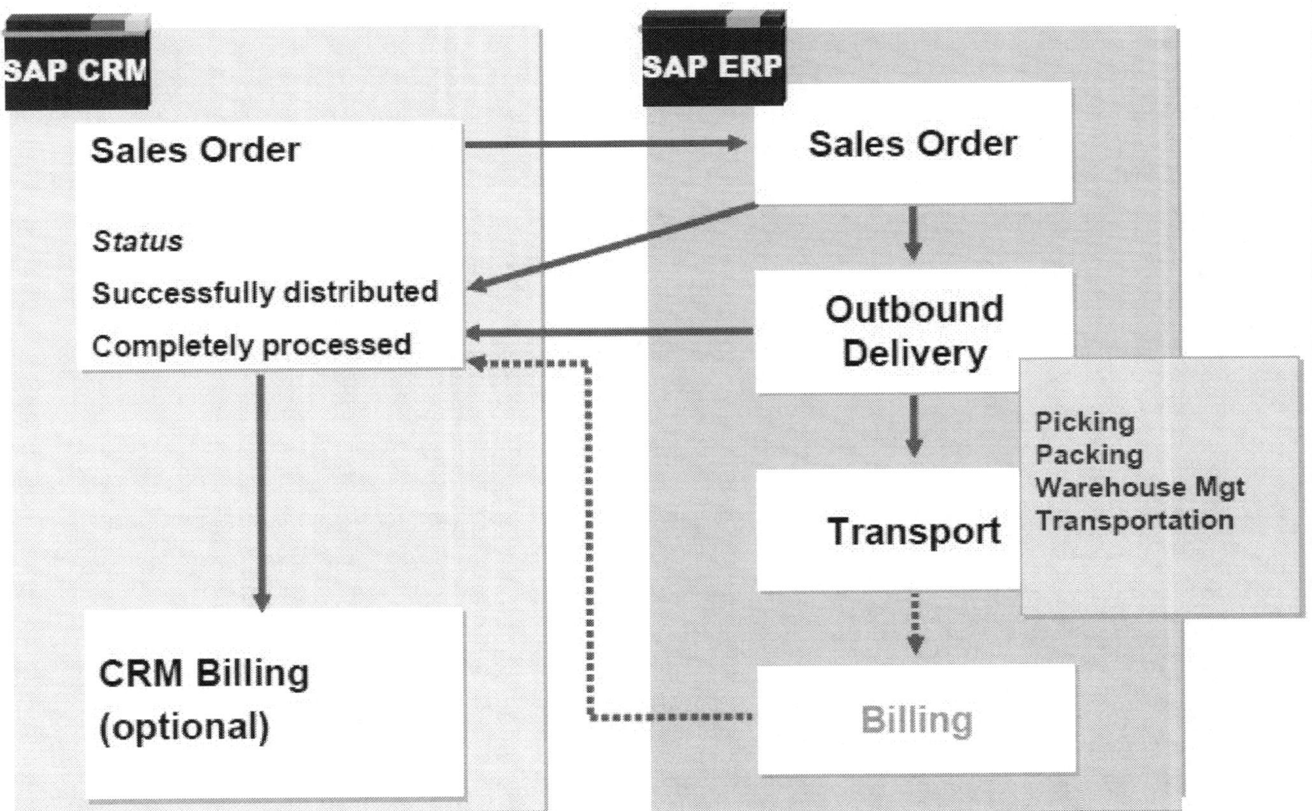

7) The SAP CRM analytics enables you to gather the relevant data and analyze it for operational and strategic decision makings. Which of the following statements are true regarding SAP CRM analytics? (Choose more than one option)

a) SAP CRM Analytics enables you to monitor and understand the customer behaviour

b) Analysis scenarios provide predefined packages and content for controlling customer focused processes

c) SAP CRM interactive reports can be used to analyze objects like activities, leads & opportunities

d) A separate BI system is required for reporting

Answer: a, b & c.

Explanation:

SAP CRM Analytics methods are used to monitor and understand the customer behaviour. The different behaviour models exist in SAP CRM. They are:

- Clustering
- Association Analysis
- Decision Tree
- Scoring
- Linear and Multi linear regression

The analysis scenarios provide predefined packages & content for controlling customer focused processes. SAP CRM compile and synchronize the data in the knowledge base and provides you the up-to date reporting tools for monitoring and measuring the success of the enterprise.

The sales environment interactive reports are generated for the objects activities like lead and opportunities. Users can conduct a search report, view a list of saved reports and searches and view reports grouped by application area.

There is no separate BI system required for reporting. Instead the SAP NetWeaver stack that comes with SAP CRM itself can be used in order to run CRM reports on the same machine.

8) Which of the following are relevant documents within the Service process of SAP CRM? (Choose more than one option)

a) Service notification

b) Billing document

c) Service Order

d) Opportunity

Answer: a & c.

Explanation:

Service process represent the complete process of the service to the customer. It is a business object which represents the service processing in the system.

Service Notification and Service Order are the related documents in the Service Process in SAP CRM.

Service Notification is a malfunction notification which represents the complaint on an object. This turns to create a Service order.

The Service order starts from assigning the objects in the service order to set status to billing request items.

Billing document and Opportunity documents are not comes under the service process.

9) Your client has a business process of providing the services for a complex objects like devices or machines to their customers. So, your client needs a complete track of all services and the objects which undergone service to each customer. Which business process do you recommend to implement in SAP CRM sales as a CRM consultant?

a) Case Management

b) Installed Base Management

c) Service Contracts

d) Knowledge Management

Answer: b.

Explanation:

Installed Base Management in SAP CRM enables the representation of objects installed at your customer's (for example, devices, machines, software and so on) for which a service is offered. It can also be used to manage objects used internally.

It is used to determine the exact object for which a problem has been reported. It is also used to identify the affected objects and its parts by the service employee. It is also used to cover the activities performed by the service contract.

Installed base Management is integrated in service processes, service contracts and Interaction center.

Case Management enables you to consolidate, manage, and process information about a complex problem. You can also use Case Management to process problems and issues that involve multiple processing steps or multiple processors. Case Management therefore supports the processing and communication flow between organizational units and helps you to increase processing efficiency.

Service Contracts are long-term agreements between companies and customers. A service contract guarantees the customer specific services within SLA (Service Level Agreement).

Knowledge Management enables the customer to research and resolve their own service problems without involving customer-service representatives.

10) You are a consultant responsible for configuring the business processes of SAP CRM Sales. What are the business processes do you identify in SAP CRM Sales? (Choose More than one option)

a) Activity Management

b) Complaint Management

c) Account & Contract management

d) Territory management

Answer: a, c & d.

Explanation:

Activity management is a key functional area of SAP CRM that administers all activities undertaken by a company's employees. It enables all relevant employees to access the necessary information saved in activities that is business activities and tasks. For example, sales representatives can use Activity Management to view the outcome of a telephone call to a customer, and sales managers can quickly and easily gain an overview of all the activities that have taken place in the department during a certain period of time.

Account and Contact management provides companies with a complete overview of their customers. It helps to obtain, monitor and reproduce all critical information such as detailed profiles, full interaction history. Sales professional are provided with a single, comprehensive view into all of the information necessary to effectively manage their sales accounts.

SAP CRM Territory Management component is specifically designed to structure and organize markets by dividing it into territories through a territory hierarchy. A country geographic structure can be mapped into Territory Hierarchy through existing Standard Attributes or Additional Attributes according to customer flavour (attributes maps Business Partner Master Data fields). Hence Business Partners will be automatically assigned to the appropriate Territory Level accordingly. Customers are able to assign a Territory Level to a Position in the Organizational Structure in order to indirectly assign the Employee Responsible assigned to that Position.

Apart from the above business process. There are other processes as below:

- Opportunity Management
- Quotation and Order Management
- Contract Management
- Incentive and Commission Management

Complaint management comes under SAP CRM service. It allows customer to create, maintain and track their own complaints and returns.

11) The client wants to launch a new campaign. The client needs the target group's segmentation. So, the client made the following statements regarding the profile, profile sets and target groups within Graphical Modeller. Which statement do you agree if you are a consultant to create the Profiles, Profile sets and target groups?

a) You can assign each Profile to different Profile sets.

b) Multiple target groups can be assigned to profile

c) A target group can be assigned to multiple profile sets

d) Each Target Group must belong to a profile set.

Answer: b.

Explanation:

The Graphical Modeller is used to create profiles, profile sets and target groups by simply dragging the attributes.

A campaign is designed to reach a specific set of target groups. It is possible only when you segment the target based on the set of characteristics.

A Profile is a finite list of characteristics and their values that make the profile of a Business Partner. A profile has to be assigned to profile set. A profile cannot be assigned to different profile sets.

A Profile Set is a type of folder for properties, target groups and sub groups. Subsets may exist in each profile set.

A target Group is a finite list of business partners that match a corresponding profiles/profile sets. It can be created manually. A target group must be assigned to a profile or profile set. A target group that is already assigned cannot be assigned to another set or profiles.

Only active target groups are can be used in marketing planner.

12) Identify the three data sources available for target group selection in SAP CRM Marketing? (Choose more than one option)

a) SAP BW Reports and Info Cubes

b) Info sets consisting of your own ABAP queries

c) SAP BCM configuration

d) Marketing attributes from the business partner master data

Answer: a, b & d.

Explanation:

There are three data sources available for target group selection in SAP CRM Marketing. They are:

- SAP BW Reports and Info Cubes
- Info sets consisting of your own ABAP Queries
- Marketing attributes from the business partner master data

The SAP BW Reports and Info Cubes allow you to select a business partner for a target group using master data, profiles or transaction data.

The Info sets from your own ABAP queries evaluate general data from the business partner master record and can be used to select target groups according to address.

You can enter marketing characteristics directly in the business partner master record. Characteristics are then grouped together, creating characteristic groups. You can edit and use them to select a target group.

You can identify the source for segmentation of target groups in the below diagram:

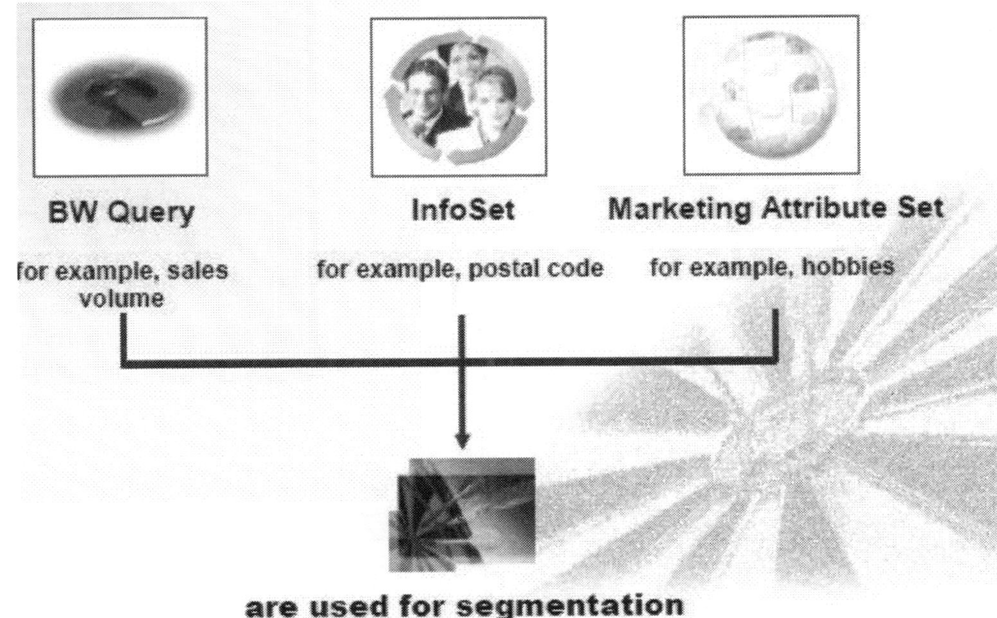

13) A profile can be assigned to only one profile set.

a) True

b) False

Answer: a.

Explanation:

A profile is a finest list of characteristics and their values that make up the "profile" of business partner.

A profile has to be assigned to profile set.

A profile cannot be assigned to different sets. A profile that is already assigned to one profile set cannot be assigned to another.

14) A Target group that is already assigned can be assigned to another profile set or profile.

a) True

b) False

Answer: b.

Explanation:

A Target group is a finest list of business partners that match a corresponding profile/ profile set. It can be created manually.

You can not assign a single Target group to multiple profile sets or profiles. Only active Target groups can be used in the Marketing groups.

15) Which planning procedure can be performed in Account planning by a Key Account Manager in the context of Trade Promotion Management?

a) Top-Down Planning

b) Bottom-Up Planning

c) Top-Bottom Planning

d) Up-Down Planning

Answer: b.

Explanation:

The SAP Trade Promotion Management application empowers account and trade managers to improve control and visibility of the entire trade promotion process. The integrated end-to-end solution enables managers to accurately plan, increase brand presence, and maximize profitability with trade activities.

The Account planning is the second step in the Trade Promotion Management, Which often involves the field representatives such as Key Account Managers (KAM) who performs "Bottom-Up" Planning procedure and gain sell-in with his accounts.

16) What is the prime use of Account and Contact Management? (Choose more than one option)

a) Detailed information on accounts

b) Quick Information on accounts

c) 360 degree view of the accounts

d) Printing of accounting view

Answer: b, c & d.

Explanation:

The following are the uses of the Account and Contact Management in SAP CRM:

- Quick and Easy to find the accounts
- Information about contact persons, companies and Relationships
- 360 degree view of accounts for the below information:
    - Interaction History

  - Activities
  - Opportunities
  - Financial and Logistical data
- Printing of account overview
- Account fact sheet

17) Identify the key Activity Management functions of SAP CRM? (Choose More than one option)

a) Ability to schedule and manage simple and complex tasks

b) Tour Planning and Activity Scheduling

c) 360 degree view of accounts

d) Bi-Directional synchronization of SAP CRM activities and calendars with Microsoft Outlook or Lotus Notes

Answer: a, b & d.

Explanation:

Key activity management capabilities of SAP CRM include:

- Ability to schedule and manage simple and complex tasks
- Ability to capture and access every customer activity, including all communication transactions, such as appointments, dates, telephone calls, e-mails, letters, meetings
- An activity journal to record, update, and track critical customer information gathered from each customer interaction, including feedback on needs and requirements, and products and services discussed. The feature also includes a user-friendly wizard, which enables sales professionals to maintain activity journals through customizable templates
- The ability to integrate many different areas of data and dynamically create a variety of surveys. For example, pharmaceutical companies could use such surveys to track the batch and product numbers of free samples offered during customer visits, while retailers could report the number of campaign costs, and other details

- Bi-directional synchronization of SAP CRM activities and calendars with Microsoft Outlook or Lotus Notes, ensuring that changes sales professionals make to their CRM calendars show up in the third-party solutions as well
- Tour Planning and Activity scheduling can be used to select business partners and create activity proposals for them which are immediately shown in the calendar.

18) What are the important components used in the Groupware integration? (Choose more than one option)

a) Groupware Connectors

b) Groupware adaptor

c) Groupware plug-in

d) Groupware severs

Answer: a & b.

Explanation:

Groupware integration is achieved by a set of Groupware Connectors and a Groupware Adapter.

The SAP Groupware Adapter on the CRM server is based on the SyncPoint technology and supports the transformation of BDoc messages to standard groupware formats (iCalendar and vCard) by using a sophisticated XSLT mapping framework called MapBox and Payload Interface (SOAP based messaging interface for exchanging data between the CRM server and groupware connector). iCalendar and vCard are the Internet standards to represent groupware calendar objects and contacts. Predefined mappings of a BDoc message to iCalendar and vCard, created using the MapBox, are delivered for groupware integration.

SAP Groupware Connectors external to the CRM server perform the message synchronization between the CRM server and the groupware server. Message transfer is performed using a reliable and open messaging interface based on XML-SOAP.

You can find the relation between these connectors in the below diagram:

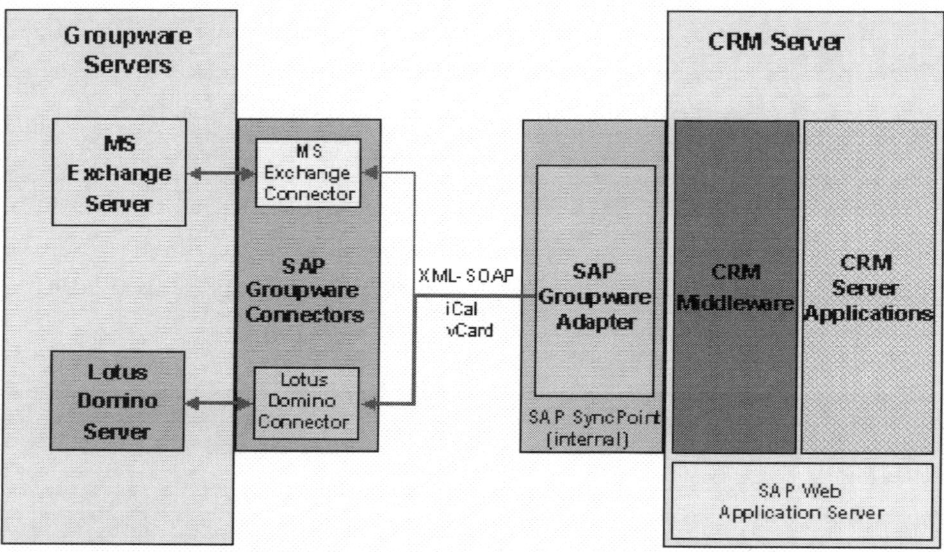

19) Identify the different chart types exist in Pipeline Performance Management (PPM). (Choose more than one option)

a) Target To Date View

b) Sales Pipeline View

c) Closing Date View

d) Sales Pipeline Change View

Answer: a, b, c & d.

Explanation:

The biggest challenge that sales professionals have is to plan and manage against the planned sales quota in an integrated, real-time application. I will introduce you to an interactive tool for sales pipeline analysis available in SAP CRM 2006s called Pipeline Performance Management (PPM). This tool was first introduced in SAP CRM on-demand in 2006, is included in SAP CRM 2006s, and will be available for subsequent releases.

PPM is built on the pre-existing business processes in SAP CRM and uses existing SAP standard sales processes in SAP CRM 2006s. PPM provides the opportunity pipeline information in the form of tables and bar charts to check won deals, expected deals, sales targets, and the remaining difference between won, expected deals, and sales targets.

There are four different chart types are offered in PPM as below:

- Target To Date View
- Sales Pipeline View
- Closing Date View
- Sales Pipeline Change View

20) You are using SAP ERP for your Contract Management System. You are now wanted to use SAP CRM as your contract Management system along with SAP ERP. There will be integration between SAP CRM and SAP ERP system. What are the actions required on integration of contracts between SAP ERP and SAP CRM? (Choose more than one option)

a) An Initial Data Transfer between SAP ERP and SAP CRM to replicate all existing contracts

b) New or changed contracts are transferred automatically from SAP ERP to SAP CRM system

c) Contracts are continually updated with the correct quantity or value in both systems

d) Sales orders can be transferred to the SAP ERP from SAP CRM

Answer: a, b & c.

Explanation:

The contract management capabilities of SAP CRM allow companies to work with customers to develop and revise customized contracts, and then submit the contracts to their customers. These contracts allow organizations to establish long-term purchasing agreements that let customers buy products under special conditions, such as lower prices or favourable delivery terms.

Integration of contracts between SAP ERP and SAP CRM:

- Contracts usually apply on a long term basis. Customers who want to use SAP CRM as their main contract management system can transfer the data from the SAP ERP system to the SAP CRM system
- You need to transfer the data from SAP ERP to SAP CRM to replicate the data in both systems
- New or changed contracts are then transferred automatically from the ERP system to the CRM system
- Contracts are continually updated with correct quantities in both systems
- In this way you can display contracts from SAP ERP in the SAP CRM system and release products from these contracts

21) Which management is used to identify the exact object for which a problem has been reported from a customer to offer the service?

a) Opportunity Management

b) Incentive and Commission Management

c) Account Management

d) Installation management

Answer: d.

Explanation:

Installation management is used to model objects installed for your customers so that you can offer services for them. It can also used to manage objects that are used internally.

Installation management identifies the exact object for which a problem has been reported. It also provides the data to the representative with information about which object is affected. It is also used to tract the activities covered by service contracts.

22) Which Component defines the attributes for the service products agreed with customer in a service contract?

a) Product level agreement

b) Business blue print

c) Service Level Agreement

d) Service order

Answer: c

Explanation:

The SLAs define the attributes (such as content, scope and means) for the service products (for example, maintenance, Hotline) agreed on with the customer in the service contract.

Using Service Level Agreements (SLAs), you work with customers to stipulate the form that the performance of a guaranteed service takes.

Parameters within the Service Level Agreement:

- Response time (technician on site within a specified time)
- Operating time/availability time (working time of the service or support center)
- Downtime (maximum number of breakdowns per year)
- Availability (assured system availability in %)
- Solution time (maximum period of time allowed for the solution of a problem)

23) In general, what are the tasks of a Service Manager in the processing cycle of a Service Order? (Choose more than one option)

a) Request a quotation for a range of services

b) Triggers billing for the customer and analyzes the complete service order

c) Checks and approves the confirmation data and decides which cost to be billed to customer

d) Carries out the work for the customer and confirms the time, material consumption

Answer: b & c

Explanation:

The following steps represents the common processing of service order:

- The customer requests a quotation for a range of services
- The Service Representative creates a quotation for services requested and communicates the same to the customer
- The Customer accepts the quotation
- The Service Representative converts the quotation into a service order and release it
- The Resource Planner assigns field service tasks to one or more of the Field Service Representatives
- The Field Service Representative carries out the work for the customer
- The Service Manager checks and approves the confirmation data and decides which cost should be billed to the customer
- The Service manager triggers billing for the customer and analyzes the complete service-order processing cycle

24) SAP CRM service orders are not replicated to SAP ERP customer service (CS)

a) True

b) False

Answer: a

Explanation:

You use service orders to record the details of a one-off service agreed upon by a service provider and a service recipient. Service order contains all the information needed to plan, execute and bill for a service.

SAP CRM service orders are not replicated to SAP ERP Customer service (CS)

25) Which billing is used for service orders, confirmations and complaints?

a) SAP SD Billing

b) SAP CRM Billing

c) SAP BI Billing

d) None of the above

Answer: b

Explanation:

If you simply want to bill CRM sales orders and are currently using SAP Sales and Distribution (SAP SD), you have the option of using either SD Billing or CRM Billing.

Billing of service contracts, service orders, confirmations or complaints, you should use CRM Billing.

Using CRM Billing, you can combine a service order item with a sales order item together in an invoice and thereby simplify communication with your customers.

CRM Billing offers a variety of output possibilities as well as automatic or manual transfer of billing document data to SAP ECC for accounting purposes. You can also analyze billing data using SAP Business Intelligence.

SAP NetWeaver Fundamentals

1) **What are the three different levels in Web Dynpro programming? (Choose more than one option)**

   a) View

   b) Controller

   c) connector

   d) Model

Answer: a, b & d.

Explanation:

Web Dynpro programming follows the Model View Controller approach which has three different levels:

- **View – Data Display**
  Views define the layout of an application. They contain the sequence and the properties of the UI elements as well as the declaration of the connection between the UI elements and the controllers
- **Controller – Interaction**
  The controller lies between the View and the Model. It formats the model data that is to be displayed in the view, processes the user entries, and returns them to the model.
- **Model – Connection to data sources and services**
  The Model forms the interface to the back end system and thus enables the Web Dynpro application to access data.

2) **What are the installation options available for SAP NetWeaver AS? (Choose more than one option)**

a) SAP NetWeaver Application server ABAP System

b) SAP NetWeaver Application server Java System

c) SAP NetWeaver Application sever ABAP and Java System

d) None of the above

Answer: a, b & c.

Explanation:

Depending on the SAP NetWeaver Application server, there are various installations are available. They are:

- **SAP NetWeaver Application Server ABAP System**

  Complete infrastructure in which ABAP based applications can be developed and used.
- **SAP NetWeaver Application Server Java System**

  Complete infrastructure for developing and using J2EE-based applications.
- **SAP NetWeaver Application Server ABAP and Java System**

  Complete infrastructure in which ABAP and J2EE based applications can be developed and used. This installation focuses on seamless Java-ABAP integration.

You can see the below picture represents the all three possible installation options:

3) What are the components of Java Cluster?

a) A Java Instance with a dispatcher and at least one server process

b) The central services, which contain a message server and an enqueue server

c) A database for the central storage of data

d) All the above

Answer: d

Explanation:

All Java components of the SAP system are known as a Java Cluster. Java clusters consist of:

- **A (central) Java Instance with a dispatcher and at least one server process**
- **The central services, which contain a message server and an enqueue server**
- **A database for the central storage of data**
- **Additional Java instances (optional)**

The client requests to SAP NetWeaver AS Java are received by the Java dispatcher. It selects a free server process the request and creates the connection between the client and the server process.

The server process runs the Java applications. The structure of server processes essentially corresponds to the structure of the Java dispatcher. The server processes are implemented a multi-thread servers and can therefore process multiple requests in parallel.

The central services run on host and form a separate Java instance. They consist of the message service and the enqueue services.

- The message service represents the infrastructure of data exchange between the nodes involved. It also provides the load balancing information for the SAP dispatcher
- The Enqueue service administers logical locks that are set in a server process by the executed application program

4) What are the basic standards are implemented for Web Services in the SAP NetWeaver Application Server? (Choose more than one option)

a) eXtensible Markup Language (XML)

b) Simple Object Access Protocol (SOAP)

c) Web Service Description Language (WSDL)

d) Universal Description, Discovery, and Integration (UDDI)

Answer: a, b, c & d.

Explanation:

The SAP Web Application Server implements the following basic Web services standards:

- eXtensible Markup Language (XML)
- Simple Object Access Protocol (SOAP)
- Web Service Definition Language (WSDL)
- Universal Description, Discovery, and Integration (UDDI)

Extensible Markup Language (XML) is a set of rules for encoding documents in machine-readable form. It is defined in the XML 1.0 Specification produced by the W3C, and several other related specifications, all gratis open standards.

Simple Object Access Protocol (SOAP) is a simple XML-based protocol to let applications exchange information over HTTP.

Web Services Description Language (WSDL) is an XML-based language that provides a model for describing Web services

Universal Description, Discovery and Integration (UDDI) is a platform-independent, Extensible Markup Language (XML)-based registry for businesses worldwide to list themselves on the Internet and a mechanism to register and locate web service applications. UDDI is an open industry initiative, sponsored by the Organization for the Advancement of Structured Information Standards (OASIS), enabling businesses to publish service listings and discover each other and define how the services or software applications interact over the Internet.

5) Which component is work as Run Time Environment in the context of SAP NetWeaver Business Process Management?

a) Process Composer

b) Process Desk

c) Process Server

d) None of the above

Answer: c.

Explanation:

The SAP NetWeaver Business Process Management (SAP NetWeaver BPM) component helps you model, execute, and monitor your business processes based on a common process model. It can help you improve the efficiency of business processes, reduce errors in complex repetitive tasks, and lower exception-handling costs.

The components are:

- **Process composer** – Enables process architects and developers to create and debug executable business process models. Each business process model clearly defines the rules and exceptions governing the process steps that are performed by people or systems in response to specific business events.
- **Process server** – Executes process models without requiring brittle translation steps between the model and code, fully integrated with the runtime technology provided by SAP NetWeaver Composition Environment.
- **Process desk** – Allows process users to perform their assigned tasks while business processes are running. Users can access context-sensitive task screens through the standard SAP user interface or through universal work lists displayed via SAP NetWeaver Portal.

6) Which is the Development tools used to develop portal contents for SAP NetWeaver Portal? (Choose more than one option)

a) SAP NW Portal Content Studio

b) SAP NW Visual Composer

c) SAP NW Developer Studio

d) SAP NW Portal Composer

Answer: a, b & c.

Explanation:

There are three development studios are available:

The SAP NW Portal Content Studio:

- Provides a central point of access and management of all portal content in the Portal Catalog tree.
- Provides a content development environment that offers content developers, of all expertise levels; the tools to create portal content without having to write code.
- Enables content to be filtered based on user access permissions.
- Provides a content development environment that enables creation of content above SAP and non-SAP applications.
- Enables multiple content objects to be edited in parallel.
- Provides backward compatibility for a variety of content developed for SAP Enterprise Portal 5.0.

The SAP NW Visual Composer:

SAP NetWeaver Visual Composer is a powerful design tool that facilitates the creation of portal content for SAP Enterprise Portal 6.0 and NetWeaver '04, using a visual user interface rather than manually writing code. It provides sophisticated, yet simple-to-use tools for creating portal iViews that process data from back-end systems.

Visual Composer operates on top of the portal, utilizing the portal's connector-framework interfaces to allow users to access a range of data sources, including SAP and third-party enterprise systems. Special connectors are also supported, such as that used for accessing data services from Siebel systems. Because Visual Composer is a fully Web-based application, business consultants can interact with business users (content experts) to build or customize pages and iViews as needed, accessing the software from any machine.

The SAP NW Developer Studio:

The Enterprise Portal perspective of the SAP NetWeaver Developer Studio enables you to do the following:

- Create a portal application project.
- Add a portal component or service to a portal application project.
- Edit the code, compile and add resources to a portal application project.
- Create a portal archive file from the portal application project.
- Upload the portal archive to a portal.

7) Which search engine is developed by SAP?

a) Google

b) MSN

c) SAPO

d) TREX

Answer: d

Explanation:

SAP NetWeaver Search and Classification (TREX) finds information in both structured and unstructured data. TREX provides SAP applications with services for searching and classifying large collections of documents and for searching and aggregating business objects.

TREX offers a flexible architecture that enables a distributed installation that is modified to different requirements. A minimal system consists of a single host that provides all TREX functions. Starting with a single-host system, you can extend TREX to be a distributed system and thus increase its capacity.

83) In SAP NetWeaver 7.0, it is compulsory to install AS JAVA?

a) True

b) False

Answer: a

Explanation:

It is compulsory to install JAVA in the SAP NetWeaver 7.0, because most of the components work with JAVA Applications.

84) Which component of SAP NW Business Warehouse server is used to read the data when a query is executed?

a) Metadata Repository

b) Data Warehousing Workbench

c) Analytical Engine

d) None of the above

Answer: c

Explanation:

There are three levels of architecture of the SAP NetWeaver Business Warehouse.

- Data Sources
- BI server
- Reporting

Metadata and Application data is managed in the Business Warehouse Server. Analytical Engine is the component which is used to read the data from the Database when a Query is executed in Business Warehouse.

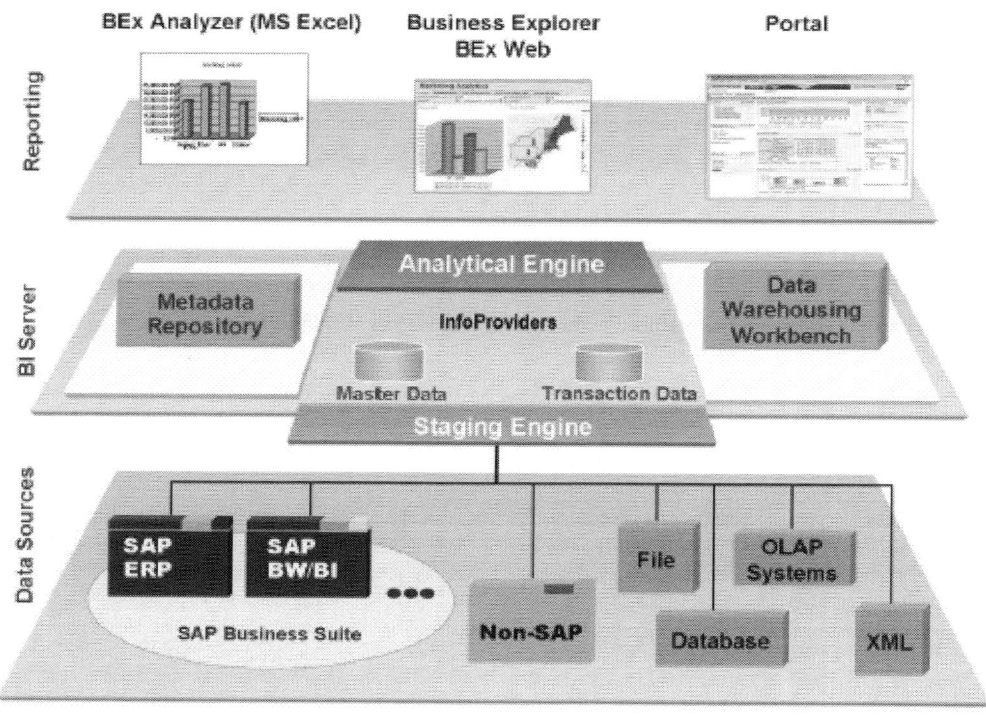

85) What is the pre-requisite for a Data Warehouse System?

a) Data modelling

b) syntax modelling

c) both a & b

d) None of the above

Answer: a

Explanation:

Data Modelling is the pre requisite for Data Warehouse System.

A data model containing key figures and characteristics are created which is used at later stage of to set up the tables in the Business Information Warehouse with master data and transaction data.

You create the data model in the following steps:

- Creating Key Figures
- Creating Characteristics
- Creating InfoCubes

86) Which tool is used for providing a familiar user interface for displaying and analyzing data in Microsoft Excel?

a) BEx Query Designer

b) BEx Information Broadcasting

c) BEx Web Analyzer

d) BEx Analyzer

Answer: d.

Explanation:

The Business Explorer Analyzer (BEx Analyzer) is the analysis and reporting tool of the Business Explorer that is embedded in Microsoft Excel.

You can call up the BEx Query Designer in the BEx Analyzer, in order to define queries. Subsequently, you can analyze the selected InfoProvider data by navigation to the query created in the Query Designer and create different query views of the data. You can add the different query views for a query or for different queries to a work book and save them there. You can save the workbook in your favourites or in your role on the BW Server.

SAP CRM Middleware

1) Which SAP system is used as a global Available-to-Promise check and demand planning solution?

a) SAP CRM

b) SAP BI

c) SAP APO

d) SAP XI

Answer: c.

Explanation:

Demand Planning (DP) is an application component in the SAP Advanced Planner and Optimizer (SAP APO) of SAP Supply Chain Management (SCM) that allows you to forecast market demand for your company's products and produce a demand plan. A consensus forecast can be reached by consolidating the inputs of marketing intelligence, promotions, and management adjustments to the statistical forecast.

2) Which component is used to communicate between CRM Middleware and CRM server applications?

a) R/3 Adapter

b) BW Adapter

c) Groupware Adapter

d) CRM Adapter

Answer: d

Explanation:

The CRM server applications exchange data with the CRM middleware via the CRM Adapter.

3) What is the transaction code for outbound queue of qRFC monitor?

a) SMOD

b) SMQ1

c) SMQ2

d) CMOD

Answer: b.

Explanation:

- SMQ1 – qRFC Monitor for the outbound queue you use this transaction to monitor the status of the LUWs in the outbound queue and restart any hanging queues manually.
- SMQ2 – qRFC Monitor for the inbound queue. You use this transaction to monitor the status of the LUWs in the outbound queue.

The Transaction codes SMOD and CMOD are used for Enhancement and Implementing of Enhancements in SAP R/3.

4) Which queues are used by the CRM to validate the data by the CRM adapter?

a) R3A* queues

b) CDB* queues

c) CSA* queues

d) CRI* queues

Answer: c

Explanation:

All queues in CRM Middleware are based on Remote Function Calls (RFCs). RFC is therefore critically important for processing in Middleware. Inbound and outbound queues are implemented using qRFC (queued RFC), although Replication & Realignment queues are based on tRFC (transactional RFC) rather than qRFC. It is also important to note that, in addition to R3A*, ISP* and

CRM_SITE* inbound queues, CSA* queues are also implemented as inbound queues as of CRM Release 4.0. Figure 8.2 shows CRM Middleware from the perspective of RFC. For all inbound queues, there is only one inbound queue scheduler.

CRM uses the CSA* queues to validate the data by the CRM adapter before subsequent processing in the other system.

5) Identify the functionalities of the CRM middleware: (Choose more than one option)

a) Data Queuing and Transport

b) Replication and realignment

c) Data Exchange and Mapping

d) CRM server applications

Answer: a, b & c.

Explanation:

There are three main functionalities provided by the CRM Middleware :

- Data queuing and Transport
- Replication and Relignment service which ensures that mobile clients or external systems obtain the data they require
- Data Exchange and Mapping

6) What are the tables involved in the context of communication between CRM system and R/3 system? (Choose more than one option)

a) CRMSUM

b) CRMCONSUM

c) CRMRFCPAR

d) CRMRFC

Answer: b & c.

Explanation:

In the R/3 system, Activate CRM as a consumer in the table CRMCONSUM and also maintain the table CRMRFCPAR. Through this table, the determination of the RFC destinations for the data transfer is connected with consumer

In the CRM system, activate R/3 OLTP as consumer the in the table CRMCONSUM.

The other two tables CRMSUM and CRMRFC are dummy tables that do not exist in the system.

7) What is the transaction code for Administration console?

e) SQ01

f) SM59

g) SMOD

h) SMOEAC

Answer: d.

Explanation:

You use the Administration Console for the administration of sites and mobiles users as well as for the administration and customizing of data distribution. You use the Administration Console for the administration of sites and mobiles users as well as for the administration and customizing of data distribution.

Replication objects are grouped together logically in publications. A publication makes one or more replication objects available to the replication. Sites can then subscribe to one or more publications in order to receive the data relevant for their work. In a mobile scenario, employees can be assigned to the company and organizations assigned to a site.

The Administration console is accessed via the transaction SMOEAC for changing site or can be accessed via the menu path “Architecture and Technology -> Middleware -> Administration -> Administration Console.

You can see the relations as below:

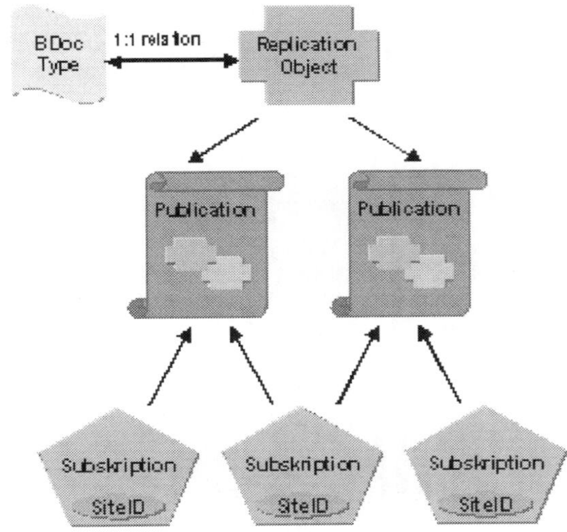

The Transaction code SQ01 is used for managing of SAP Queries

The Transaction code SMOD is used for Enhancement of Objects in R/3

The Transaction code SM59 is to create and maintain RFC connections in R/3

8) What is the transaction to monitor the Transactional RFC (tRFC)?

a) SARFC

b) SMQ1

c) SMGW

d) SM58

Answer: d.

Explanation:

This Transaction lists only those transactional RFCs that could not be carried out successfully or that had to be planned as batch jobs. The list includes the LUW ID and an error message. Error messages displayed in SM58 are taken from the target system. To display the text of the message, double-click on the message.

Transaction SM58 also lets you control your transactional RFC at various stages. If the call ends abnormally during the sending process, you may need to use the *Rollback LUW* function to manually rollback the LUW before attempting a resend. If the target system was unavailable, you can use the *Backgr.job* function to display the batch job created for your call. *Execute funct. Module* lets you restart the call after the occurrence of a temporary error (such as a syntax error).

The transaction code SMQ1 is used for outbound queues

The transaction SMGW is used to determining the parameters for gateway with the Gateway Monitor transaction.

9) All customizing adapters are assigned to object class CUSTOMIZING?

a) True

b) False

Answer: a

Explanation:

For several customizing objects, there is a predefined data transfer from R/3 to CRM available, even if the structure of the customizing tables are different in R/3 and CRM. The data of one or more data base tables are grouped in customizing Adapter Objects. The data of customzing adapter obejct can be transffered from R/3 to CRM system with an initial load.

You can use the download monitor to control the initial load.

All customizing adapter objects are assigned to object class CUSTOMIZING

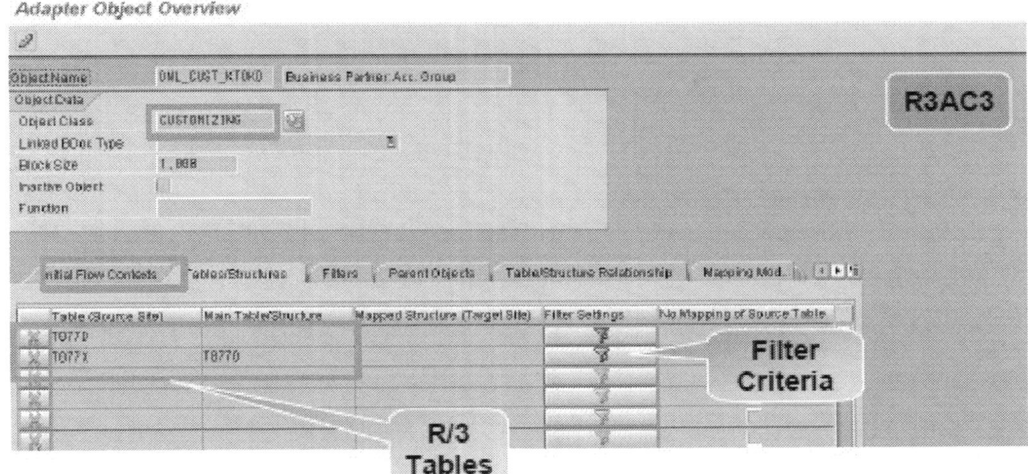

10) What is the naming convention for the qRFC queues used in the initial load when the data request is sent from the CRM system to the R/3 Backend?

a) R3AI<Customizing Adapter Object>

b) CDB<Customizing Adapter Object>

c) CSA<Customizing Adapter Object>

d) CRI<Customizing Adapter Object>

Answer: a

Explanation:

The naming convention R3AI<Customizing Adapter Object> is used for the qRFC queues in the initial load of Customizing adapter object.

You can see in the below diagram:

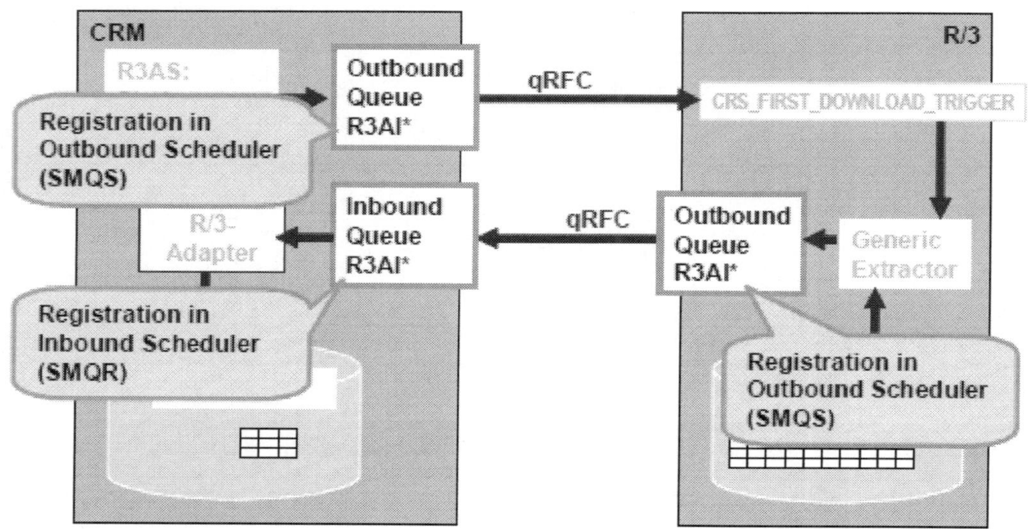

"R3A" represents R/3 Adapter and "I" represents Initial Load.

The other qRFC naming conventions are used as follows: These are used in Outbound Queues

CDB* is used for loads from CRM to CDB (Consolidated Database)
CSA* is used for CRM server Applications

CRI* is used in loads from CRM to CDB in Inbound Queues.

11) What is the transaction code for CRM BDoc Modeller?

a) SMQS

b) SBDM

c) ST05

d) SE11

Answer: b.

Explanation:

The BDoc Modeller is a tool used for displaying, creating and enhancing BDoc types.

The transaction code SBDM is used for this purpose.

The transaction code SMQS is used for registration of outbound scheduler in CRM

The transaction code ST05 is used for performance analysis in SAP R/3

The Transaction code SE11 is used for ABAP dictionary in SAP R/3.

12) What are the transactions used to activate the mass data processing in the CRM system? (Choose more than one option)

a) R3AC1

b) R3AC2

c) R3AC5

d) R3AC4

Answer: a & c.

Explanation:

If there is a mass updating of data from SAP R/3 to SAP CRM, You can use the Mass data processing in CRM.

There are two transactions R3AC1 and R3AC5 used to activate mass data processing in the CRM system. Along with this activity, you have to follow the following steps in mass data processing:

- Maintain the CRMOBJECTHIER table in CRM system and in ERP Back end system.
- Modify the table CRMMASSUPD to allow activation for each adapter object
- You must register the MASS* inbound queue in Transaction SMQR
- You must start the CRM0_BUNDLE_AND_START_QUEUES report to send the data to the CRM system after you execute the changes in the ERP back end.

You can see a pictorial representation:

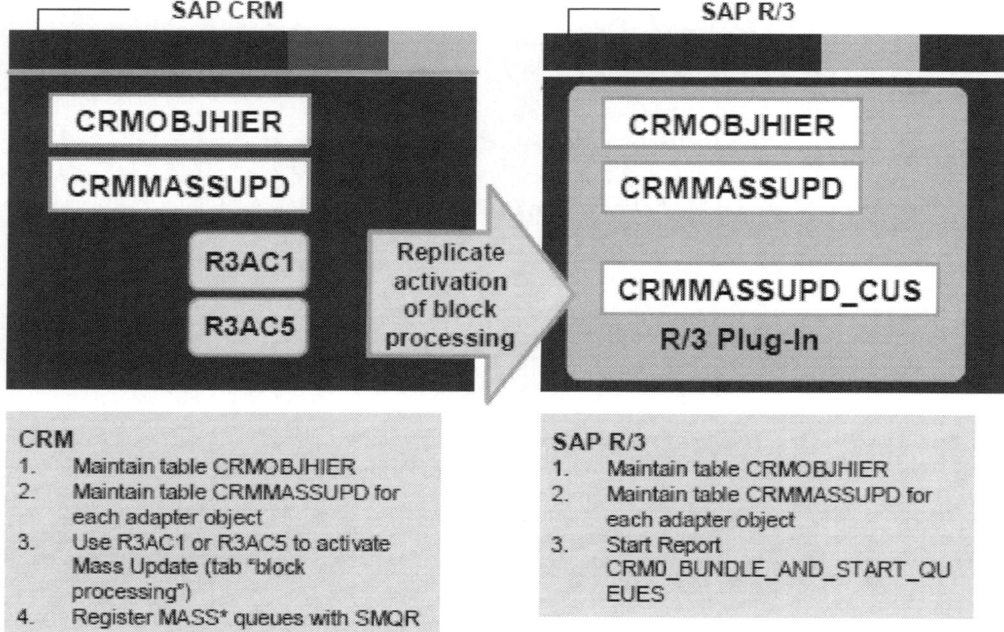

13) Which processing is the better choice when the data is transferred from SAP CRM to SAP Business Connector?

a) SOAP/XML processing

b) IDOC Processing

c) Direct processing

d) None of the above

Answer: b

Explanation:

SAP Business Connector is a rebranded licence version of WebMethods Integration Server provided by SAP as a middleware solution for their R/3 products.

IDOC processing is the best choice when you transfer the data from CRM to the SAP Business connector. Because, IDOC transfer is quicker in comparison to SOAP/XML processing. The IDOC document contains no metadata information and therefore the size of the document sent down the line in substantially smaller in comparison.

You can see in below diagram:

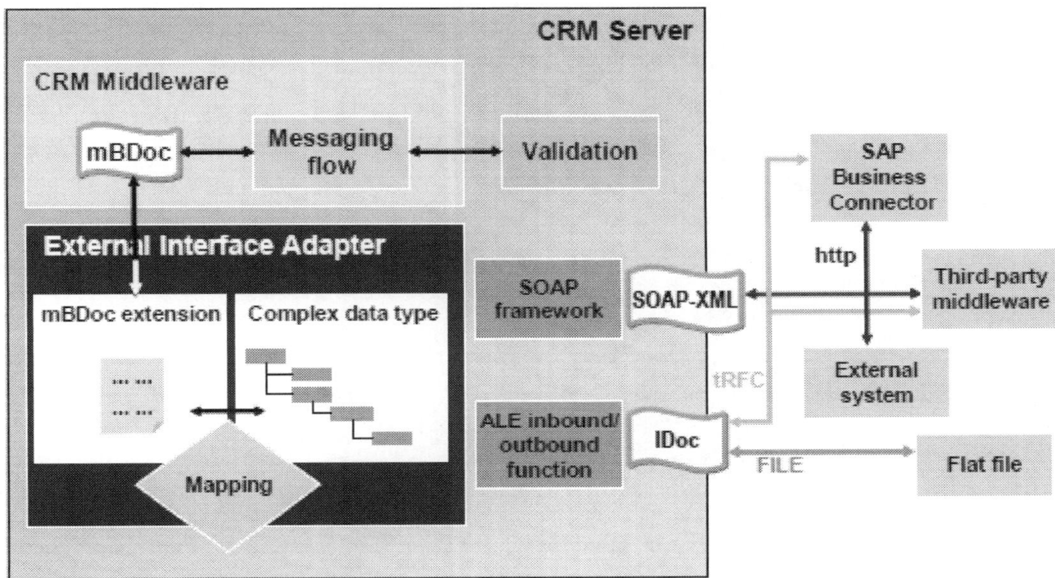

14) What are the two background processes have to be scheduled for running CRM Middleware Monitoring Cockpit? (Choose more than one option)

a) SMWP_COCKPIT

b) SMWP_BATCH

c) SMWP_GE

d) SMWP_GE_BATCH

Answer: b & d.

Explanation:

The CRM Monitoring Cockpit provides you with status information and also serves as a navigation platform to access important administration and monitoring tools in CRM Middleware.

The pre-requisite for running CRM Middleware Cockpit is to schedule the two background process:

- SMWP_BATCH: to update the displayed runtime information
- SMWP_GE_BATCH: to update the generation information

The reason for scheduling these two background processes is that the runtime information needs to be updated more frequently than the design time information.

The other two options SMWP_COCKPIT and SMWP_GE do not exist in the system. So, they are not suitable.

CRM User Interface

1) Identify the ways how a business role can be assigned? (Choose more than one option)

a) By using the User Parameter CRM_UI_PROFILE in your user master record

b) A user's assignment in the organizational model

c) By using the authorization SAP_ALL

d) The PFCG role a user maintained for his user master record that correspond to the PFCG role in Business Role Customizing

Answer: a, b & d.

Explanation:

The Business Role is a role describing the user interface of SAP CRM and displays the CRM functions in the form of BSP applications in the CRM Web Client.

Defining a Business role influences the complete content visible to a user assigned to the role:

- Navigation Bar
- Layouts
- Authorizations
- Available applications
- Entry page content

A user can be assigned to multiple Business roles

There are 3 ways how a business role is assigned:

- By using the user parameter CRM_UI_PROFILE in the user master record

  You can assign a business role to a user in the transaction SU01 (User Master Record) with the parameter CRM_UI_PROFILE

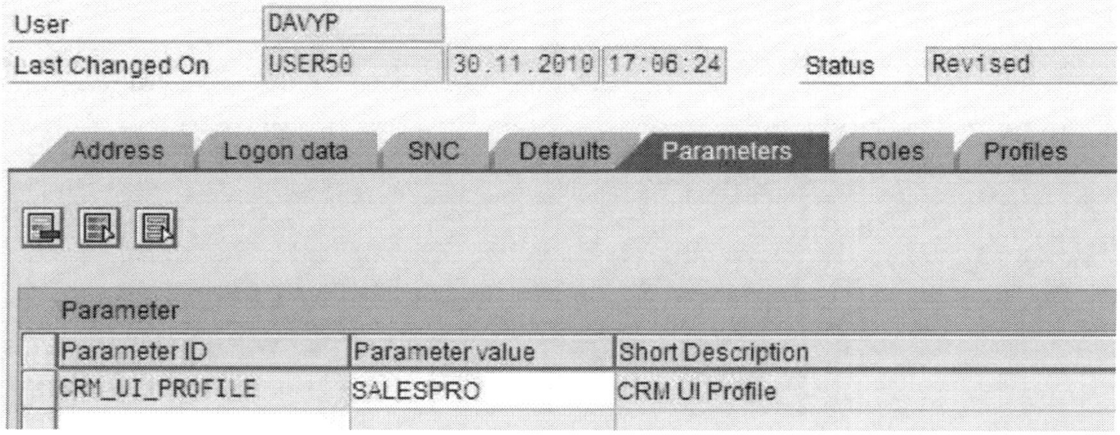

- A user's assignment in the orgnizational model

  The Business role is assigned to an orgnaizational position in the organizational model and the user is assigned to a organizational position

Display Business Role

Position: Agent CP US — IC Agent CP US

Planning Status: Active

Validity: 30.11.2010 to 31.12.9999 — Display change infor

Business Role

Business Role: SALESPRO

Record 1 of 1

- The PFCG role a user maintained for his user master record that correspond to the PFCG role in Business Role Customizing

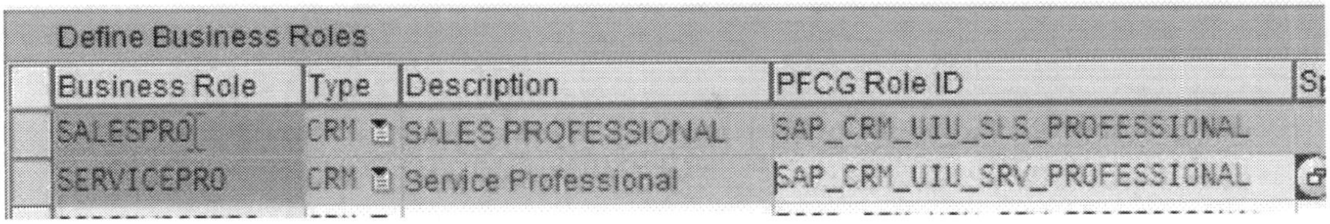

Define Business Roles

Business Role	Type	Description	PFCG Role ID	S
SALESPRO	CRM	SALES PROFESSIONAL	SAP_CRM_UIU_SLS_PROFESSIONAL	
SERVICEPRO	CRM	Service Professional	SAP_CRM_UIU_SRV_PROFESSIONAL	

2) Which Report is used to determine the Business role assigned to a particular user?

a) CRMD_UI_ROLE_PREPARE

b) CRM_UI_PROFILE

c) CRMD_UI_ROLE_ASSIGN

d) None of the above

Answer: c.

Explanation:

The Report CRMD_UI_ROLE_ASSIGN is used to determine the Business role assigned to a particular user. Based on the Business Role, the PFCG profiles are determined and assigned.

The Report CRMD_UI_ROLE_PREPARE is used to create the role menu file based on the settings in Customizing.

CRM_UI_PROFILE is only a parameter used for authorization. It is not a report.

The below flow chart explains the usages of each report and transaction in respect of Business Role:

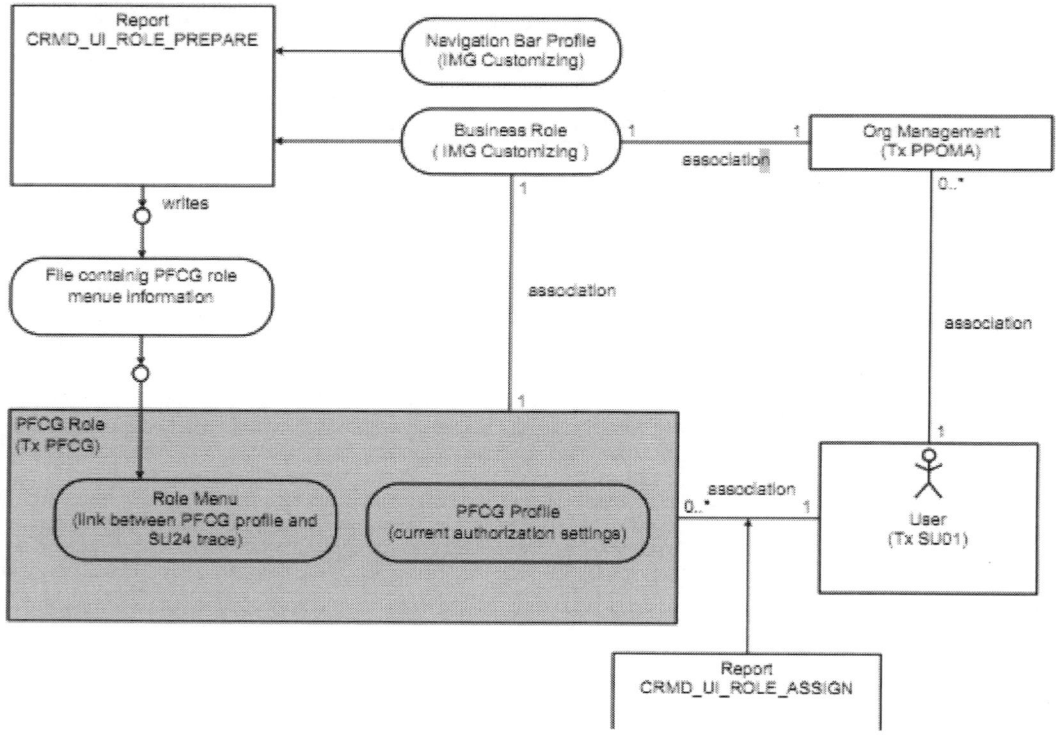

3) Identify the different types of links that can be integrated to Navigation Bar? (Choose more than one option)

a) Link

b) Work Center

c) Launch Transaction

d) BI Report

Answer: a, b, c & d

Explanation:

Navigation Bar provides links and available business content for a user.

There are four different types of links that can be integrated to Navigation Bar.

Link: It opens a CRM applicationwhich can be a search or a creation page.
Work Center: Opens a work center page.
Launch Transaction: You can integrate other web pages via the transaction launcher.
BI Report: You can define logical links for any existing BI report.

You can see in the below diagram:

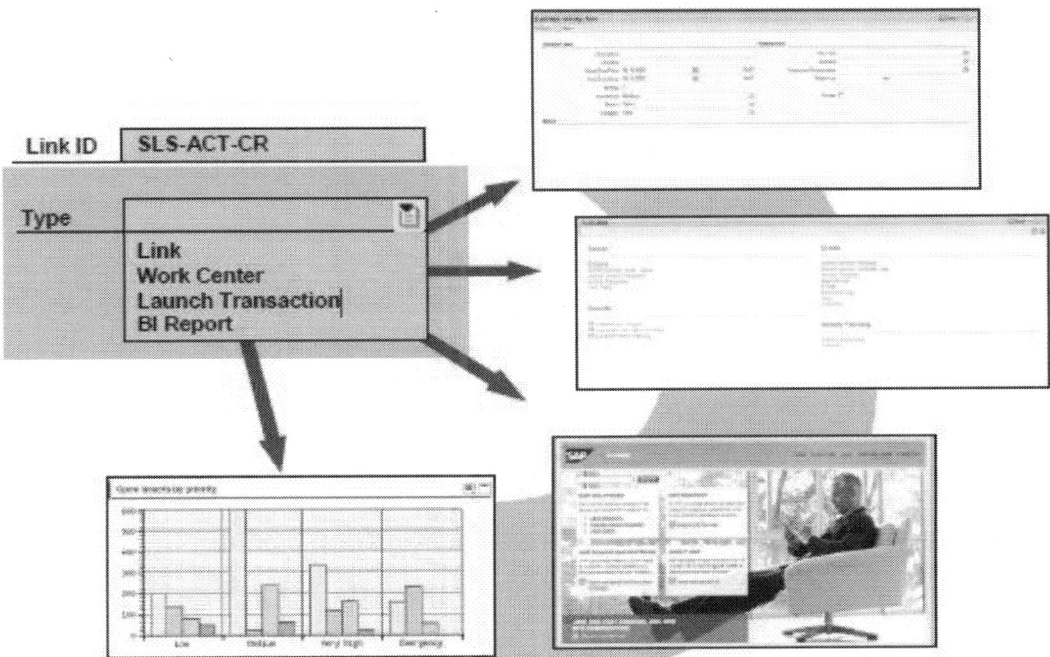

4) **You are required to call the transaction for an R/3 Sales order through transaction launcher in CRM. Which transaction launcher type can be used?**

a) BOR-Transaction

b) BI-Transaction

c) URL-Transaction

d) None of the above

Answer: a.

Explanation:

The transaction Launcher supports two types of transactions.

- BOR Transaction
- URL Transaction

Any SAP system transactions are integrated in BOR (Business Object Repository) transactions. So, The SAP sales order transaction can be called through BOR Transaction.

You can find the below diagram for your reference:

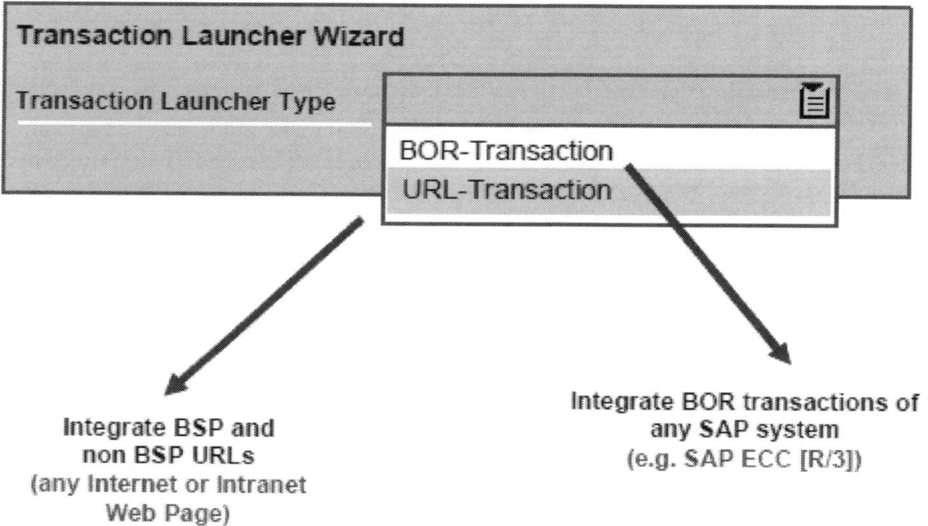

The BI-Transaction type does not exist in the system.

5) Which component is responsible for rendering the output and relevant UI controls in a Model View Controller?

a) Model

b) View

c) Controller

d) None of the above

Answer: b.

Explanation:

In a Model View Controller (MVC),

The View handles the Visual output. It is responsible for rendering the output and relevant UI controls like data fields and push buttons. All output is received from the controller for rendering.

The Controller the interaction logic and provides the connection between a view and a model of a MVC application. A controller receives all key board and mouse input from the view.

The Model consist of contexts nodes that links the fields of a view to the underlying business layer (BOL). Each Data field on a view visualizes an attribute of a context node.

You can see the data flow and control flow of a MVC application in the below diagram:

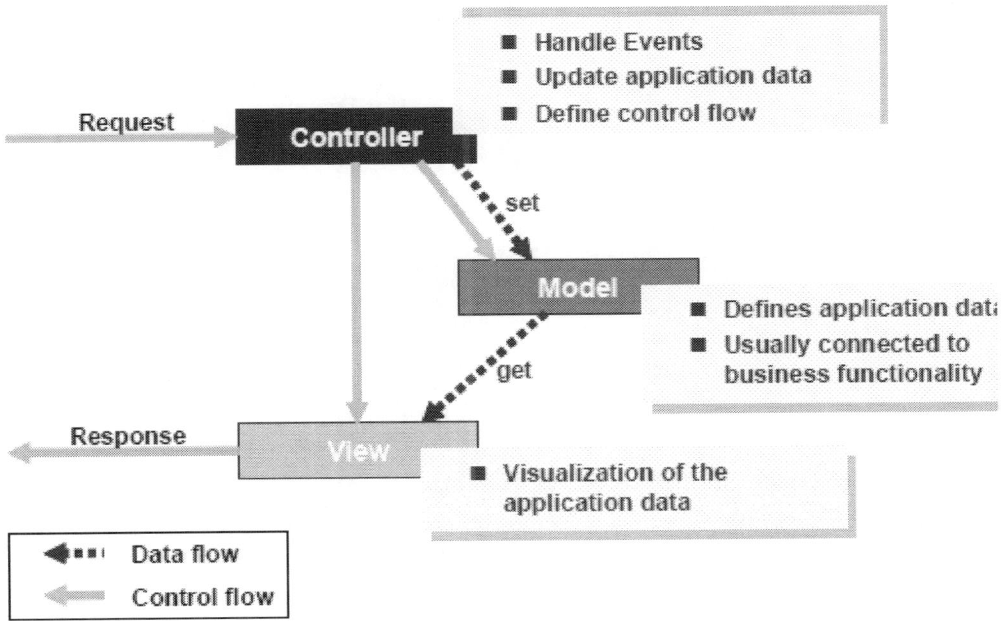

6) **What is the Transaction code for BSP Component Workbench?**

a) CRMC_UI_PROFILE

b) BSP_WD_CMPWB

c) PFCG

d) SU01

Answer: b

Explanation:

The Transaction BSP_WD_CMPWB is used to display the all development objects of the CRM Web Client applications.

The Transaction CRMC_UI_PROFILE is used to define Business Role directly

The Transaction PFCG is used to maintain the authorization profiles.

The Transaction SU01 is used for maintain the master data.

7) Which of the following is part of the CRM landscape? (Choose More than one option)

a) Interaction Center

b) ERP

c) BI

d) SCM

Answer: a, b, c & d.

Explanation:

The SAP CRM solution is the sum of all CRM functions and incorporates CRM components as well as the components SAP Business Intelligence (SAP BI), Supply Chain Management (SAP SCM) and SAP ERP (SAP ECC or SAP R/3)

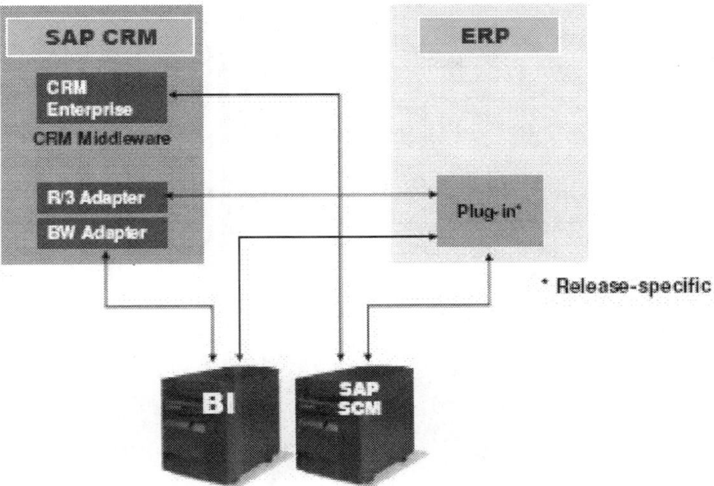

8) **Which components map the data between the APIs and the Business Object Layer?**

a) Controller

b) Generic Interaction Layer

c) View

d) Business Engine

Answer: a.

Explanation:

Generic Interaction Layer components map the data between Business Object Layer and Application Programming Interfaces (APIs). The mapping is necessary as every CRM object needs to expose its data model in a defined way in order to handled by the Business Layer.

You can see the below figure illustrate the relation between different layers:

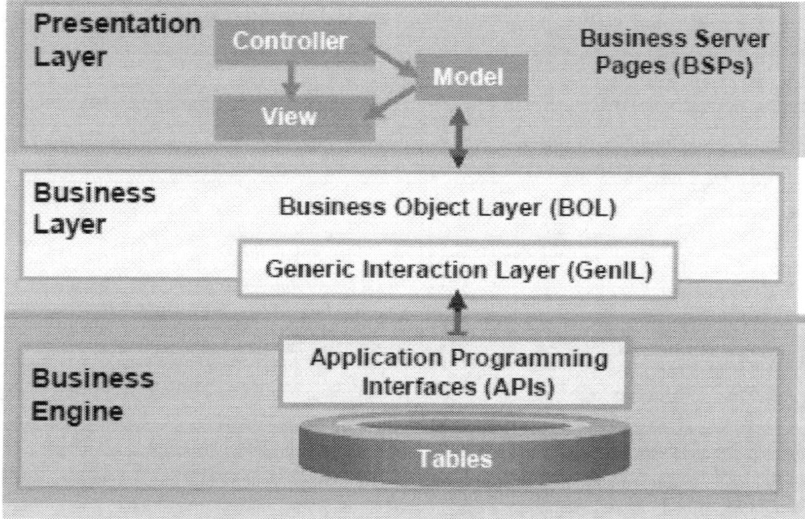

9) Each root object is also an access object in the context of Business objects.

a) True

b) False

Answer: a

Explanation:

Business object is the smallest unit of an object model. Each BO is assigned a unique name. The structure is either defined in the ABAP dictionary or directly in the GNEIL Component.

An access object is a special type of Business Object whose ID can be used to determine both the attributes of the access object itself and those of its dependent object.

The Root object is the only object within the hierarchical structure of a data model that is assigned as superior object to all other objects.

Each Root object is also an Access object.

10) What is the IMG path for defining layout profile components?

e) Customer Relationship Management -> Business Role -> Define Layout Components

f) Customer Relationship Management -> UI Framework -> UI Framework definition -> Define Layout Components

g) Customer Relationship Management -> UI Framework -> Technical Role Definition -> Define Layout Components

h) None of the above

Answer: c

Explanation:

The Layout Components are defined in the IMG Path:

Customer Relationship Management -> UI Framework -> Technical Role Definition -> Define Layout Components.

The Layout Profile defines the Navigation Frame of the CRM Web Client. The navigation frame can be used to define the header area, footer area, work area, and navigation bar.

11) Which tool is used to configure the views that are position fields, remove fields, rename labels?

a) PFCG and Report

b) Easy Enhancement Workbench

c) Web Service tool

d) UI configuration tool

Answer: d

Explanation:

UI configruation tool is used configure views:Position fields/columns, add and remove fields/ columns from the field list, rename fields..etc.

PFCG tool is used for define authorizations

Web Service tool is used for Create Web Services

Easy Enhancement Workbench tool is used create customer-specific fields.

12) What is the functionality used to integrate a link to an external Web page to the CRM Web Client UI application of some of your users.

a) Link

b) Transaction Launcher

c) Work Center

d) None of the above

Answer: b.

Explanation:

You have to use the transaction Launcher to integrate the link to an external Web page to the CRM Web UI Client.

First, you have to define a URL ID in customizing with the following IMG path:

Depending on the release, it can be located at:

Customer Relationship Management -> UI Framework -> Technical Role Definition -> Transaction Launcher -> Define URLs and Parameters

Or

Customer Relationship Management -> Interaction Center Web Client -> Basis Functions -> Transaction Launcher -> Define URLs and parameters

Then use the Transaction Launcher (Wizard) in order to generate information that can be integrated into the CRM Web UI using below IMG Path

Customer Relationship Management -> UI Framework -> Technical Role Definition -> Configure Transaction Launcher

13) What is the IMG path for Designer Layer Customizing?

a) customer Relationship Management -> Business Role -> Maintain design layer

b) Customer Relationship Management -> CRM Cross-Application Components -> Maintain design layer

c) customer Relationship Management -> UI Framework -> UI Framework definition -> Maintain design layer

d) All the above

Answer: c.

Explanation:

Design layer is used for changing several UI components at one time. Design Layer logically positioned between the BSP Layer and the BOL Layer.

The following activities can be achieved through Design Layer Customizing:

- You can set the Field Visibility
- You can Rename Field Labels
- You can Assign Value Help from Dictionary

Design Layer Customizing can be achieved by the following IMG Path:

Customer Relationship Management -> UI Framework -> UI Framework definition -> Maintain design layer

You can see the design Layer as below:

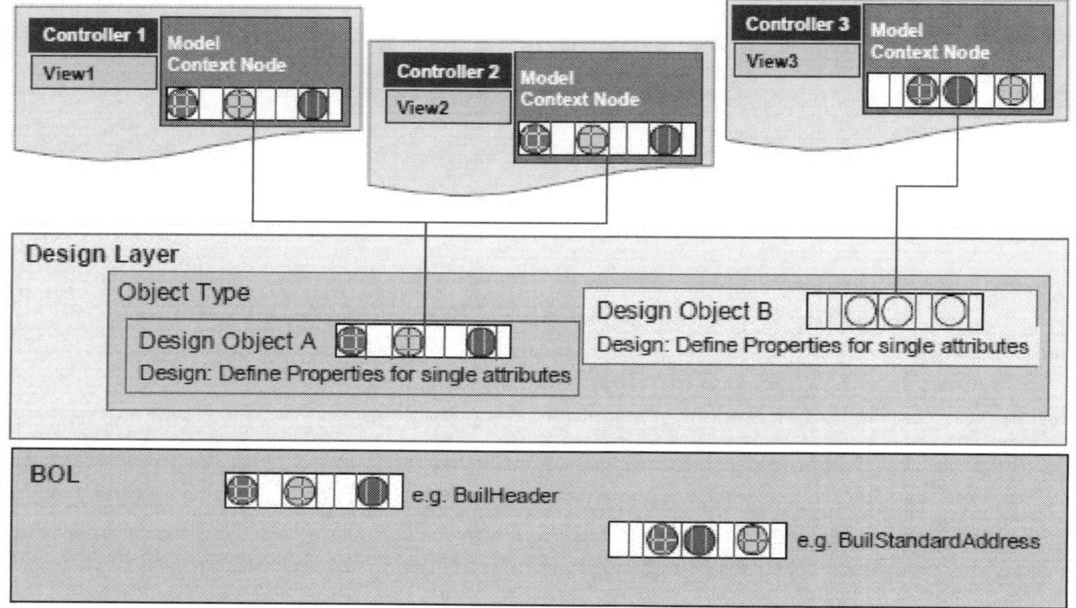

14) The CRM Web client has an L-Shape frame. Which of the following are components of the L-Shape? (Choose more than one option)

a) Work Area

b) System Links

c) Navigation Bar

d) History

Answer: a, b, c & d.

Explanation:

The L-shape provides easy global *navigation* throughout the entire SAP CRM application. The L-shape is static in position and size. It covers the upper and left-hand parts of the screen. The L-shape consists of the header area and the navigation area.

Header area	The header area is located at the top of the screen and provides generic shortcuts and

	special functions.
Navigation area	The navigation area contains primary navigation through the SAP CRM application and options for directly triggering creation of often-used objects.

Please find the snapshot of CRM web client.

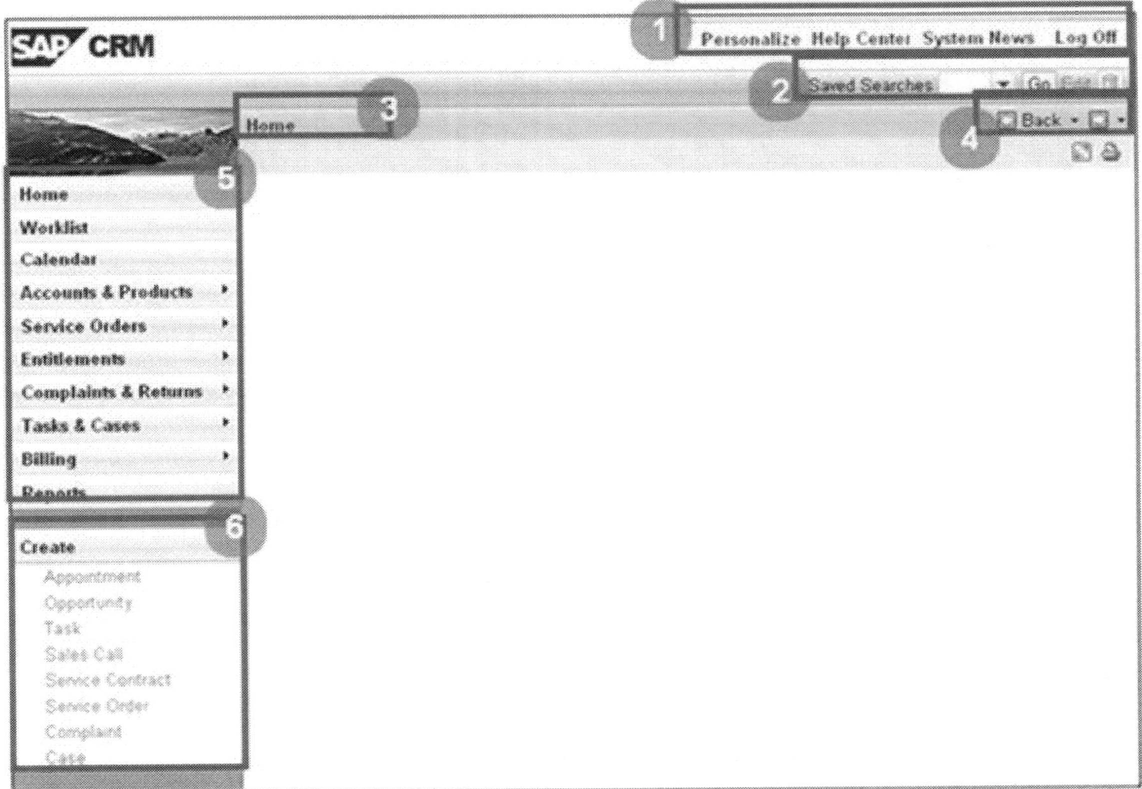

The option which are available in both Header area and Navigation area,

1. System links
2. Saved searches
3. Work area title

4. History back and forward
5. Navigation bar
6. Quick create links

15) Which tool is used to extend the business objects in SAP CRM with User defined fields?

a) Design Layer Customizing

b) BSP component Workbench

c) Easy Enhancement Workbench

d) Cascading Style Sheets customizing

Answer: c.

Explanation:

The Easy Enhancement Workbench allows you to enhance business objects in the SAP CRM with user-defined fields and tables and distribute them to SAP ECC and the Mobile Client via the CRM Middleware.

The Easy Enhancement Workbench can be accessed via Transaction Code EEWB

The system landscape must be set up in order to be able to use system-wide generation.

You can see the structure of Easy Enhacement Workbench:

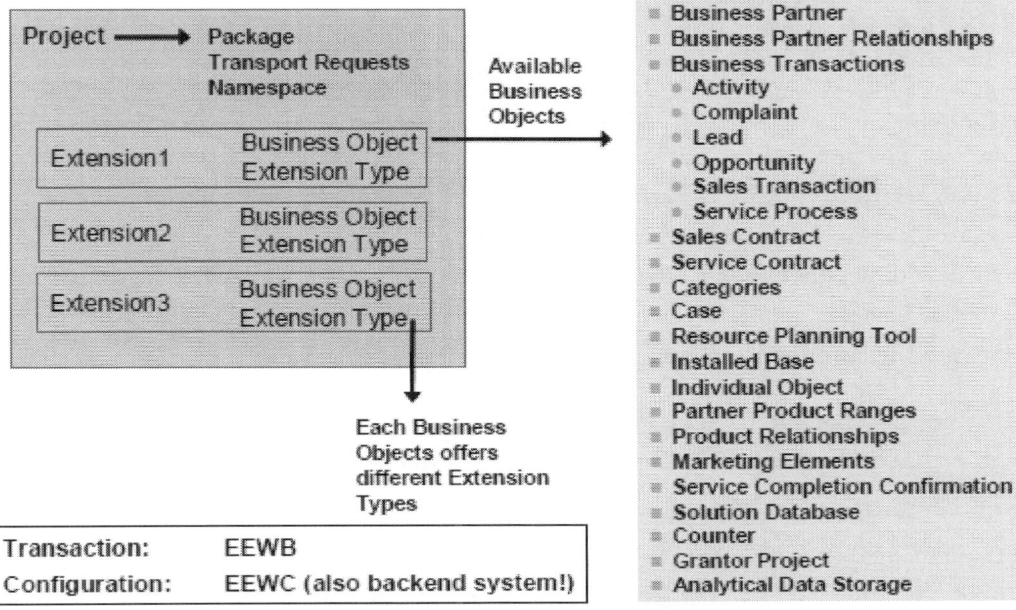

Below are the some of the Tools and their tasks:

Tools	Tasks
UI Configuration Tool	Configure Views: Add or Remove or Position the fields/Columns
UI configuration Tool and Fact Sheet Customizing	Configure Fact Sheet
Easy Enhancement Workbench	Create Customer Specific fields
Design Layer Customizing	Assign value helps / dropdown list boxes from DDIC customer specific fields
.CSS (Cascading Style Sheets) customizing	Create own skin
PFCG and Reports	Define Authorizations
Web Service Tool	Create Web Service

16) Which code is generated when you save the settings in the runtime repository editor in the component work bench?

a) C

b) C++

c) HTML

d) XML

Answer: d.

Explanation:

The Runtime Repository Editor shows the runtime repository of a UI component. In the runtime repository, you can see and edit the view set composition, that is, which views are assigned to a view area and which view areas belong to a view set. In this runtime repository, you can also see and edit the navigational links between the views of a UI component. You can see the component interface description and the component usages.

The Component Workbench therefore offers an editor that visualizes the existing XML coding and offers an easy maintenance of the different elements in the Runtime Repository.

17) You need to create an enhancement set before you can start to enhance a component and assign it to a client. What is the view used to create an enhancement set?

a) BSPWDV_EHSET_ASG

b) BSPWDV_CMP_EXT

c) BSP_WD_CMPWB

d) None of the above

Answer: b.

Explanation:

An Enhancement set is a folder for enhancements that belong together. You need to create an enhancement set before you start to enhance a component.

You use the transaction code SM34 to create an enhancement set.

You have to use the View Cluster BSPWDVC_CMP_EXT to create an enhancement set.

You need to assign the enhancement set to the client. This can be achieved by the transaction SM30 and the view BSPWDV_EHSET_ASG.

The pictorial representation is as below:

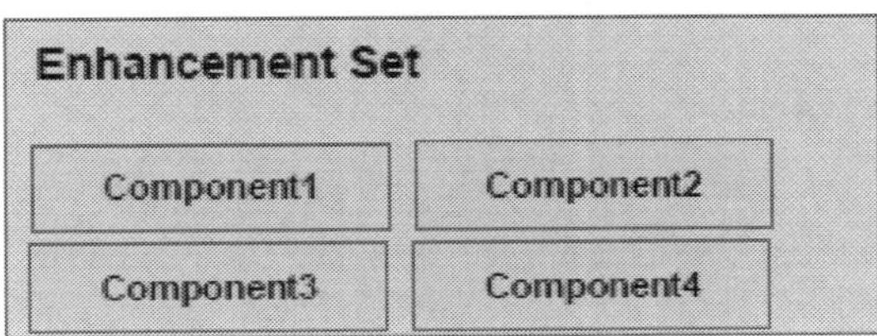

An enhancement set is a folder for enhancements that belong together

1) Create Enhancement Set
   - Transaction: SM34
   - View Cluster: BSPWDVC_CMP_EXT

Enhancement Set ZCUSTOPP

2) Assign Enhancement to Client
   - Transaction: SM30
   - View: BSPWDV_EHSET_ASG

Client	No	Enhancement Set
800	1	ZCUSTBP
	2	ZCUSTOPP

The option BSP_WD_CMPWB is a transaction for a component workbench where you can edit the UI components.

18) The Data retrieval from the data base to the BOL can be tested with the BOL browser. What is the transaction code to access the BOL browser?

a) GENIL_MODEL _BROWSER

b) GENIL_BOL_BROSWER

c) BROWSER_BOL

d) All the above

Answer: b.

Explanation:

The Transaction code GENIL_BOL_BROWSER is used to access the BOL browser.

The Transaction Code GENIL_MODEL_BROWSER is used to access the MODEL browser.

The Transaction Code BROWSER_BOL does not exist in the system.

19) What is the main layout file of the CRM UI Web Client?

c) Thtmlb_visuals_stand.css

d) Thtmlb_rtl_stand.css

e) Thtmlb_stand.css

f) Thtmlb_IE7_stand.css

Answer: c.

Explanation:

Below are the some of the CSS (Cascading Style sets) and its usages:

File Name	Description
thtmlb_stand.css	The main layout of the CRM UI Web client. Each skin has its own version of this file. This style sheet contains all the styles that users typically change, Such as references to background pictures and colours. The majority of the styles defined in this style sheet are additions to those defined in the Core style sheet. Only in cases where a certain skin deviates greatly in structure will it overwrite the core style.
thtmlb_visuals_stand.css	Each skin has its own version of this file. This style sheet contains additional styles that are needed When you want to create visual effects (for example, hover effects for buttons and links). Visual effects can be deactivated centrally, so the styles within this style sheet are only needed if visual effects are activated.
	Right-to-left support. RTL is automatically

thtmlb_rtl_stand.css	managed by the browser, but in some cases the flow needs to be changed manually in the CSS file.
Thtmlb_IE7_stand.css	Each skin has its own versions of these files. These are browser specific skins.
thtmlb_core_stand.css	This is the basic style sheet that is used by all skins. It is one of the two style sheets that only exist in one version for all skins. The content of it is the structural CSS used mainly for layout purposes. You have the option of creating a new skin with a copy of this style sheet, but we recommend that you do not make changes to this file as this could result in a displacement within THTMLB UI controls.

20) The change of existing skins is a manual work. What is the sequence of steps to change the existing skins?

a) Copy Skin to local files -> Connect to CRM Server -> Edit Skin locally -> Make Skin Available

b) Make Skin Available -> Copy Skin to local files -> Edit Skin locally -> Connect to CRM Server

c) Connect to CRM Server -> Copy Skin to local files -> Edit Skin locally -> Make Skin Available

d) Connect to CRM Server -> Edit Skin locally -> Make Skin Available -> Copy Skin to local files

Answer: c.

Explanation:

There are four steps to change the skins. The change of existing skins is a manual work and not yet supported by system tools.

Step 1: You can access the Cascading files directly on the CRM server by connecting with your local PC to the CRM server via web DAV.

Step 2: You create a copy of an existing skin to local file.

Step 3: You can change the colours and the size of the different elements.

Step 4: Later you can either store the file on your local PC or upload the files back to the CRM Server.

You can see the pictorial representation as below:

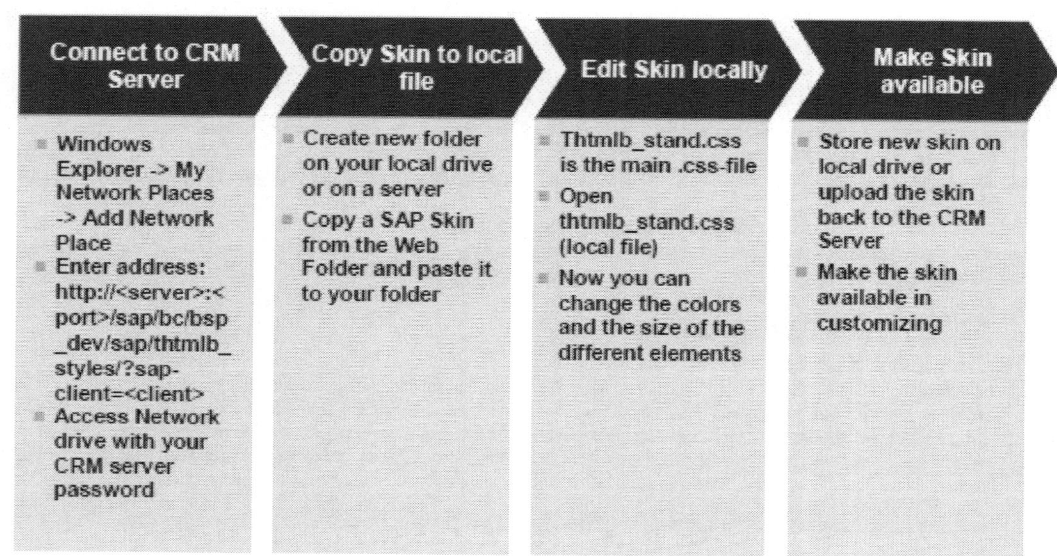

All available skins are stored in the table CRMC_THTMLB_SKIN in CRM system.

21) CRM Middleware requires additional software and an additional server

a) True

b) False

Answer: b

Explanation:

As of SAP ECC 6.0, the plug-in will be contained directly in SAP ECC. Until SAP ECC 6.0 the plug-in is delivered separately and has to be installed. Hence CRM Middleware doesn't require any addition software.

22) Which status of the service object indicates active use of service interface that cannot be changed?

a) Draft

b) Productive

c) Active

d) Not Productive

Answer: b.

Explanation:

There are four states of the service object. They are:

- **Draft:** This is the initial status of service object. You can edit the object. Objects are saved and can be enhanced later on.
- **Active:** Web Services created and available for testing and WSDL export. Object changes are permitted by setting the status back to draft. The objects are overwritten automatically during the next activation
- **Productive:** This status indicates the active use of the interface. Object cannot be changed but you can copy the object
- **Not Productive:** Status indicates that service is not used. Object can be set back to productive. It can be deleted or copied

You can find the graphical representation of the flow of status of the service object:

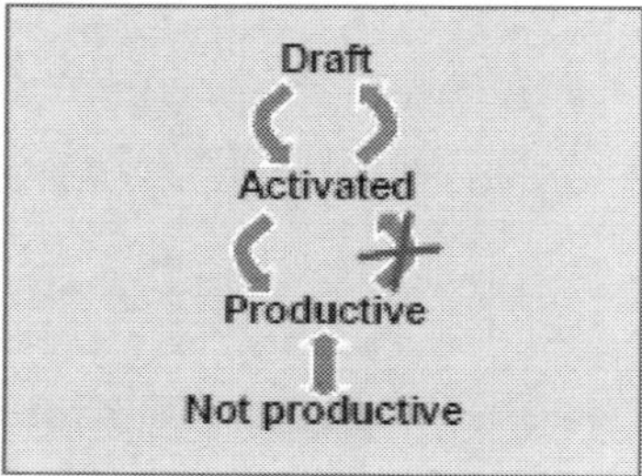

23) Which component is used to exchange data between views?

a) Component Controller

b) Views

c) View sets

d) Custom Controller

Answer: d.

Explanation:

Custom Controller is used to exchange data between views.

Views contains the input fields that you see in a browser

View sets are the group of views that have common characteristics

Component controller acts as data interface to the outside. Inside it share the data with the Custom controller.

Runtime Repository is a file that contains all information about the elements within the component.

You can see below the graphical representation of the overview of UI components:

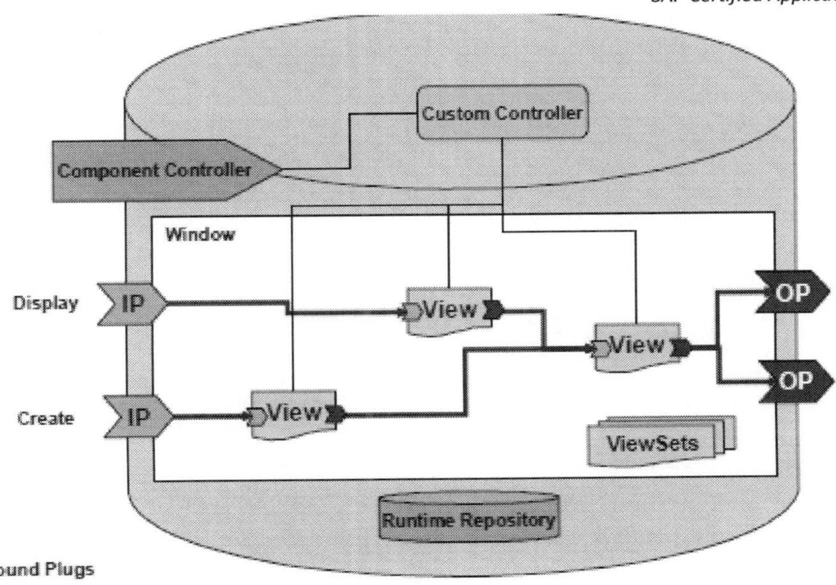
Custom Controller
Component Controller
Window
Display
IP
View
View
OP
OP
Create
IP
View
ViewSets
Runtime Repository
Inbound Plugs
Outbound Plugs
Navigational Links

SAP CRM Interaction Channels

1) Identify the channels that come under the SAP CRM Web channels? (Choose more than option)

a) E-Marketing

b) E-Service

c) E-Commerce

d) Web Channel Analytics

Answer: a, b, C & d.

Explanation:

SAP CRM enables a complete range of Web channel processes, including:

- **E-marketing**
    - Support demand generation and customer loyalty processes via the Internet.
    - Personalize your customers' Web experiences with the most relevant and convenient online interactions and information.
- **E-commerce**
    - Run business-to-consumer (B2C) or business-to-business (B2B) selling processes on the Internet.
    - Enable a full range of online selling processes, including quote and order management, pricing and contracts, interactive selling and configuration, web auctions, and selling via partners.
    - Streamline sales and fulfilment operations with an end-to-end order-to-cash process.
- **E-service**
    - Offer your customers an intuitive channel to perform service tasks, from requesting a service visit to logging a complaint or registering a product.
    - Enable customers to perform service-related tasks such as checking order status, obtaining order tracking information, managing accounts and payments, and researching and resolving product problems.
    - Service complex products that require sophisticated maintenance.
- **Web channel analytics**

- Gain insight into, analyze, and act on e-business trends.
- Measure and optimize the success of your Web shop and online content.
- Perform analysis across the breadth of marketing, sales, and service from a Web perspective, and track and use Web behaviour to target customers and drive future marketing activities.

2) What is meant by Request Management in the context of E-Service?

a) Enables the web customers to obtain quotations and place orders for products

b) Enables companies to provide online pricing tailored to each customer

c) Enables customers to research and resolve their own service problems

d) Provides customers to create and update service requests and to check their status

Answer: d.

Explanation:

Request Management provides Internet customers with a tool to create and update service requests and to check their status. Customers can use this to select the most convenient appointment time for a field service visit.

Apart from Request Management, there are other facilities available in E-service:

- Knowledge Management
- Live Customer Support
- Customer service
- Complaints and Returns management

3) Which business area of Partner Channel Management enables to better recruit, ramp-up and manage the channel partners?

a) Partner Order Management

b) Channel Marketing

c) Partner Management

d) Partner and Channel Analytics

Answer: c

Explanation:

SAP CRM provides a Web-based application to manage partner relationships and enable channel partners to sell more effectively.

There are 6 main business areas exist in the SAP Partner Channel Management:

- **Partner management**
    - Manage channel partner relationships throughout the entire partner life cycle.
    - Recruit new partners, plan and forecast channel sales and revenues, segment your partner base for more effective partner programs and management, and manage partner compensation plans, and track partner training and certifications.
- **Channel marketing**
    - Motivate partners to sell your products and services rather than competitive offerings.
    - Provide relevant information to partners, maintain consistent branding, engage in joint marketing campaigns with partners, and manage channel marketing funds and partner incentives.
    - Use functionality to manage content, catalos, collateral, campaigns, and leads – as well as personalization features and a partner locator – to drive demand for your products through channel partners.
- **Channel sales**
    - Give your partners and direct sales force the same knowledge, tools, and expert advice.
    - Gain insight into demand across all selling channels to effectively forecast future business.
    - Enable a full range of channel sales processes, including account and contact management, activity management, opportunity management, deal registration, and pipeline forecasting.
- **Partner order management**

  - Optimize partner ordering processes and include partners in collaborative selling across organizational boundaries.
  - Enable a complete set of channel order management processes including quote and order management, interactive selling and configuration, pricing and contracts, and point of sale (POS) and channel inventory management.
  - Empower end customers to order products and services across your demand network and support distributed, order-management scenarios.
- **Channel service**
  - Ensure consistent and timely service to end customers by providing your partners with the tools and expertise to manage problem resolution and ongoing service relationships.
  - Enable a range of channel service business processes, including knowledge management, service resource planning, service order management, live partner support, warranty management, and complaints and returns management.
- **Partner and channel analytics**
  - Get a broad range of standard reports and analyses to determine partner coverage and gaps, partner and channel performance, revenue and sales statistics, the return on your partner investments, your gross margins with partners, and partner utilization.
  - Provide channel partners with reports and analyses relevant to their business.

4) Which Portal serves as an interface for employees and partners?

a) The Partner Portal

b) The Channel Manager Portal

c) Both a & b

d) None of the above

Answer: a.

Explanation:

The Partner Portal serves as a user interface for employees and partners.

The Partner Portal provided with the tools and information to more effectively sell to and do business with end customers. It supports self-service, relevant information, content, transactions and analyzes for partners.

There are two groups of employees who access the partner portal:

- Partner Managers
- Partner Employees

The Channel Manager Portal enables your organization to manage partner relationships, collaborate with channel partners, and optimize channel operations.

5) Which Functional area of SAP CRM channel management incorporates partners into your E-commerce?

a) Price Management

b) Channel Commerce

c) Knowledge Management

d) None of the above

Answer: b.

Explanation:

Channel Commerce Incorporate partners in to your E-Commerce strategy and enable collaborative selling across organizational boundaries.

It enables your company:

- To Incorporate channel partners into E-Commerce platform to process customer sales
- Facilitate a single, consistent face to the customer over the internet
- To maintain the end customer relationships

The E-commerce provides the following advantages:

- Collaborative showroom
- Distributed content and catalog management

- Distributed order management

The other options are Price management and Knowledge management comes under the other functional areas like E-Selling and E-Service.

6) Which tool is used to manage the large number of incoming emails in the Interaction Center Management?

a) Interactive Scripting

b) Intent Driven Interaction

c) E-mail Response Management System (ERMS)

d) Call list management

Answer: c.

Explanation:

E-mail Response Management System (ERMS) is a tool used for manage large amount of incoming emails. It provides services for automatically processing and organizing incoming emails.

It provides tools for agents to efficiently and consistently respond to messages and for managers to administer, monitor, and report on the whole email process.

SAP delivers the pre-configured ERMS settings and functions that you can extend using custom coding.

Interactive scripting allows managers to design the step by step scripts and allow agents to execute these scripts whenever they need guidance for the customer interaction.

Intent Driven Interaction (IDI) supports rule based agent guidance and ensures that customer interactions are handled according to corporate standards via rule based alerts.

7) What is the use of the component "The scratch pad" in the interaction center?

a) Shows most relevant information about the current interaction

b) Shows alerts for the agents by the alert modeler

c) Contains push buttons for the telephony functions

d) Allows agents to write down notes

Answer: d

Explanation:

The below are the components of the interaction center screen:

The Scratch pad allows agents to write down notes that can be added to the business documents at any time.

Account Information shows the most relevant information about the current interaction like customer name and company.

The alerts generated by alert modeller are displayed for the agents.

Communication information shows information from the communication management software.

The tool bar contains pushbuttons for the telephony functions.

The Work area processes the business transactions. Start the call lists, scripts or perform detailed search for business partners.

The navigation area enables agents to start the transactions and navigate between different screens.

You can see the pictorial representation below:

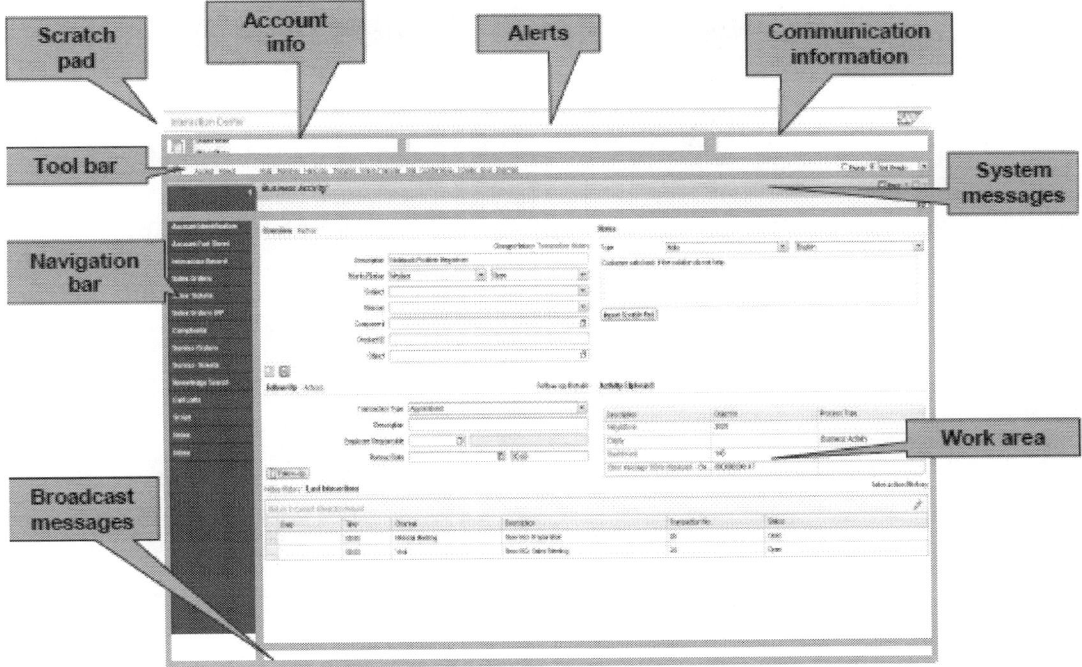

8) What is the use of Activity Management with mobile sales?

a) Provides companies with a complete overview of their customers and interested parties

b) Allows sales representatives and managers to allocate resources for daily tasks

c) Provides sales order processing

d) None of the above

Answer: b.

Explanation:

This business scenario seamlessly connects all the business processes that typically occur during a sales cycle and makes the information available to anyone in the sales team.
The Activities component is an essential component of the Mobile Sales application and supports sales representatives in organizing their daily work. In addition, it also provides a sales manager

with a fast and clear-cut overview of all the activities that are to take place or have taken place in the sales organization over a particular period.

Account and Contact management provides companies with a complete overview of their customers and interested parties. It helps to obtain, monitor and reduce all the critical information.

Order and Quotation management with mobile sales provides sales order processing functions that companies can use to configure products, determining pricing, create proposals...etc.

9) You use administration console for the administration of sites. What are the components generated automatically when you save your site definition for mobile clients? (Choose more than one option)

a) Site ID

b) Outbound Queue

c) Inbound Queue

d) Outbound IDOC

Answer: a, b & c.

Explanation:

You use administration console for the administration of sites and mobile users as well as for the administration and customizing of data distribution.

You have to create one site per mobile client within the administration console. Depending up on the business process you assign subscriptions to the site. Subscription is an optional. You can also assign employees and organizations to simplify the maintenance.

When saving your site definition, a site ID, an inbound and outbound queue is created automatically.

You can see the pictorial representation below:

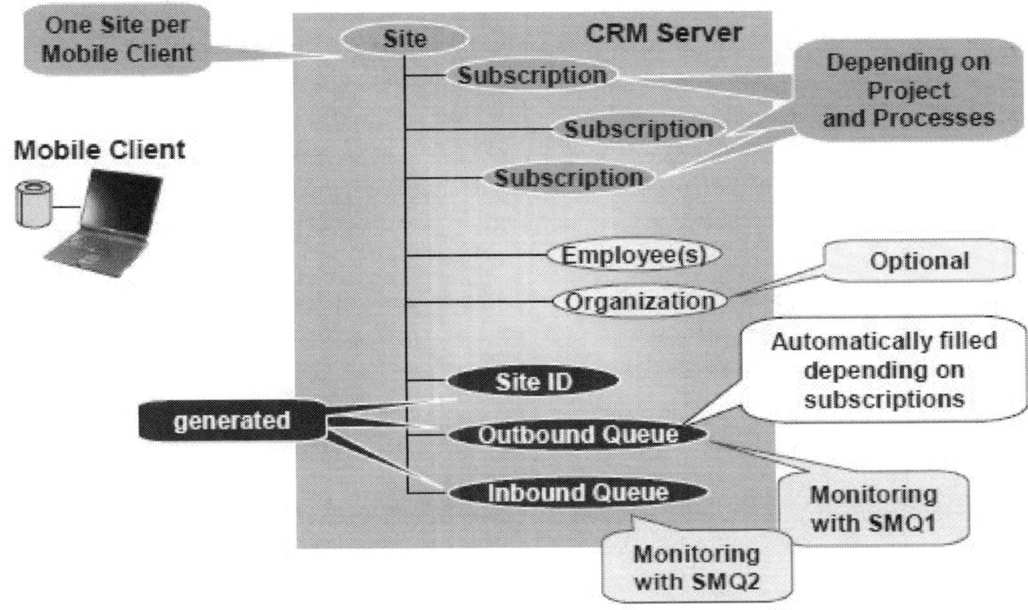

10) Where will we install the Mobile Application Studio (MAS)?

a) Mobile Application Repository

b) Mobile Application Repository Server

c) Mobile Development Work Stations

d) All the above

Answer: c

Explanation:

Mobile Application Studio (MAS) is an object-oriented, visual development tool that is tailored to the architecture of SAP mobile client applications. It allows you to customize mobile client applications, delivered by SAP, according to your specific business requirements, or develop your own applications.

Mobile Application Studio (MAS) must be installed on all Mobile Development Workstations (MDWs) where application developers customize, test and generate mobile client applications.

The metadata of a mobile client application is delivered as the Mobile Application Repository (MAR). This repository must be installed on the Mobile Repository Server (MRS) for each environment. Application developers working on individual MDWs establish a connection with the MAR from MAS.

MAS is integrated with Microsoft Visual Studio .NET and provide a set of visual modelling tools to facilitate application development as well as a code generator.

11) Which component is required to be installed on mobile devices that work with the mobile sales for handheld applications?

a) SAP Mobile Engine

b) Mobile Application Repository

c) Microsoft Visual Studio

d) None of the above

Answer: a.

Explanation:

The SAP Mobile Engine is installed locally on a mobile device and is equipped with a Web server, a database layer and its own business logic. Staff working remotely can therefore work offline and do not have to wait for a network connection to complete time-critical business applications. The SAP ME offers tools for synchronization and data replication that make the data of the mobile device consistent with that of the backend.

SAP Mobile Engine equipped with a java virtual machine and offers an open programming model with which mobile applications can be developed. This open system architecture makes the platform independent of both the mobile devices and network and supports mobile devices such as personal digital assistants, laptops and smart phones.

Mobile application repository can be used in the context of Mobile Application studio.

12) What is the use of copy controls in the creation of transaction types?

a) Used to create new transactions

b) Used for Business Add-on

c) Used to create follow up documents

d) Used for creation of tables

Answer: c.

Explanation:

A transaction type controls processing of a specific business transaction like creating a new transaction type for an opportunity.

Copy controls are used to copy the data into the follow up documents. You have to maintain the copy controls for header and item level.

13) What are the Field Applications available in SAP CRM? (Choose More than one option)

a) Mobile Sales

b) Mobile Service

c) Mobile Sales for Handhelds

d) Mobile Service for Handhelds

Answer: a, b, c & d.

Explanation:

SAP CRM Field Applications comprises the following applications:

- Mobile Sales
- Mobile Services

- Mobile Sales for Handhelds
- Mobile Services for Handhelds

14) In the case of customer analytics, you use Churn Analysis to retain the customer. In order to work with churn analysis, there should be integration between the different systems. What are the systems involved in churn analysis? (Choose more than one option)

a) SAP CRM

b) SAP BW

c) SAP SRM

d) SAP R/3

Answer: a, b & d.

Explanation:

You can use the Churn Analysis to analyze your customers' churn behaviour to understand it better and to be able to predict other customers' likelihood to churn. This understanding allows you to take counter-measures against customer churn. In this way, you can reduce the churn among your most valuable customers and increase customer retention in the long term.

In the process flow of the churn analysis the below systems are involved:

- SAP CRM
- SAP R/3
- SAP BW

These three systems provide the information and process the churn analysis as below:

- System provides customer master data and marketing attributes (SAP CRM)
- System provides the profitability data (SAP R/3)
- System updates data in the customer knowledge base (SAP BW)
- Identify active and lost customers (SAP BW)
- Predict active customers likelihood to churn based on past data (SAP BW)
- Determine value of active customers for the company (SAP BW)
- Determine and understand profile of valuable at risk customers (SAP BW)
- Transfer analytical results (SAP BW)
- System updates the customer churn information (SAP CRM)

You can see the pictorial representation as below:

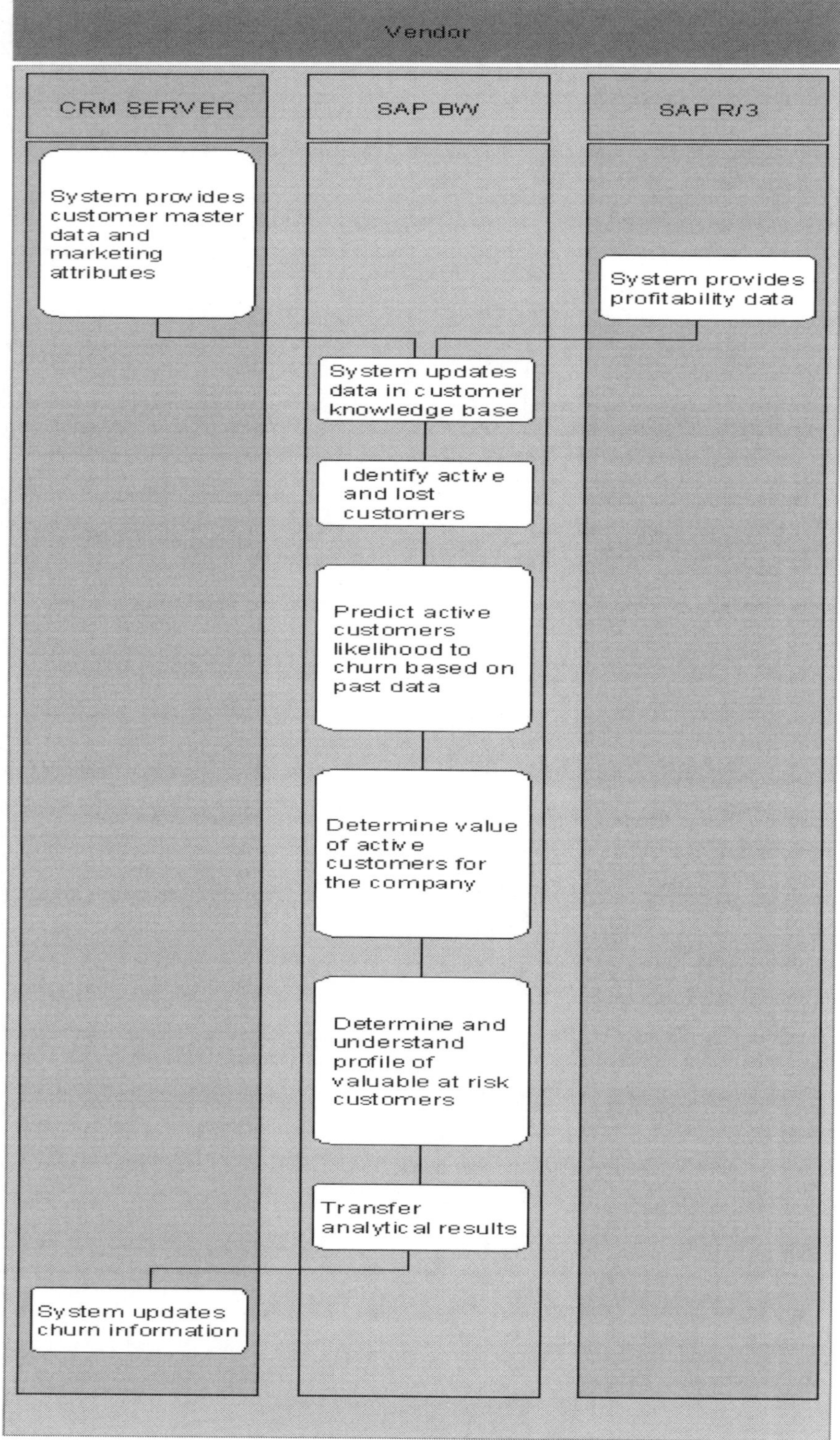
Vendor
CRM SERVER
SAP BW
SAP R/3
System provides customer master data and marketing attributes
System provides profitability data
System updates data in customer knowledge base
Identify active and lost customers
Predict active customers likelihood to churn based on past data
Determine value of active customers for the company
Determine and understand profile of valuable at risk customers
Transfer analytical results
System updates churn information

15) What are the functions can be performed with the Knowledge Management process in CRM system? (Choose more than one option)

a) Managing CRM documents

b) Managing News

c) Lead Management

d) Clustering

Answer: a & b.

Explanation:

Knowledge Management is used to store the documents and News. This means it is used to manage the following functions in CRM:

- Managing CRM documents
- Managing News

You can format documents and make them available for third parties to read, as well as make them available to an approver for checking. This additional quality assurance improves the content of your published documents. This in turn increases the acceptance and readiness of the user –your target group- to read the published documents.

His process helps you to make current news available to your users in a simple way. Additionally, you can offer your user's further information and a link to Business Objects.

Lead Management is designed to help automate the initial pre-sales process, freeing up your sales department to focus on the most valuable prospects and opportunities.

Clustering is a technique used for customer segmentation.

16) "Campaign Planning" is used to plan your key figures in campaign. Which analytics covers Campaign planning"?

a) Customer Analytics

b) Product Analytics

c) Marketing Analytics

d) Sales Analytics

Answer: c.

Explanation:

Campaign planning comes under Marketing Analytics. You can use this business process to plan your key figures for a campaign. When you are planning a campaign, you need to be able to analyze your data and predict what the outcome would be under certain circumstances. Key figures from SAP SEM allow you to do this. The Marketing Planner is directly connected to SAP SEM and SAP BW to allow in-place analysis of your campaign data. You can simulate whether you are able to supply, for example, and then adjust your planning accordingly.

There are a variety of ways in which you can use SAP SEM planning and SAP BW reporting to optimize your campaign.

- You can plan the distribution of products available to the customers or business partners available.
- You can analyze the success of your campaign and use this for future campaign planning.
- You can plan the costs and how you wish to distribute your budget amongst your customers. You can then check your budget to simulate whether this will work and if necessary, adjust your figures to get the best possible value from your marketing activities.
- You can carry out a what-if analysis and determine what the return on investment would be from your campaign.

Apart from campaign planning there are some other Marketing Analytics available in CRM. They are:

- Marketing Budget Planning
- Target Group Optimization
- External List Analysis

17) Where can you create or copy the campaigns and campaign elements?

a) Customer Planner

b) Marketing Planner

c) Allocation Planning

d) E-mail Campaign

Answer: b

Explanation:

Campaigns and campaign elements are created or copied in the Marketing Planner which can either be accessed directly or via the Marketing Calendar. The Marketing Planner allows you to carry out all of the necessary steps for planning a campaign, right up to the point where you execute the campaign. All of this information is updated in SAP SEM and SAP BW for reporting purposes.

The Marketing Calendar is the first point of entry for setting up your actual campaign. You can use it to get an overview of all your campaigns so that you can see where/if they overlap and from here, you can link your campaign to related promotions. You can also create new campaigns or promotions directly from this screen.

Allocation planning is a further tool available that allows you to determine how you are going to distribute a set number of resources to the people that you wish to contact.

E-mail campaign is one type of campaign. It is not a tool to create a campaign. Customer Planner does not exist in the context of Campaign.

You can see the process flow image of campaign as below:

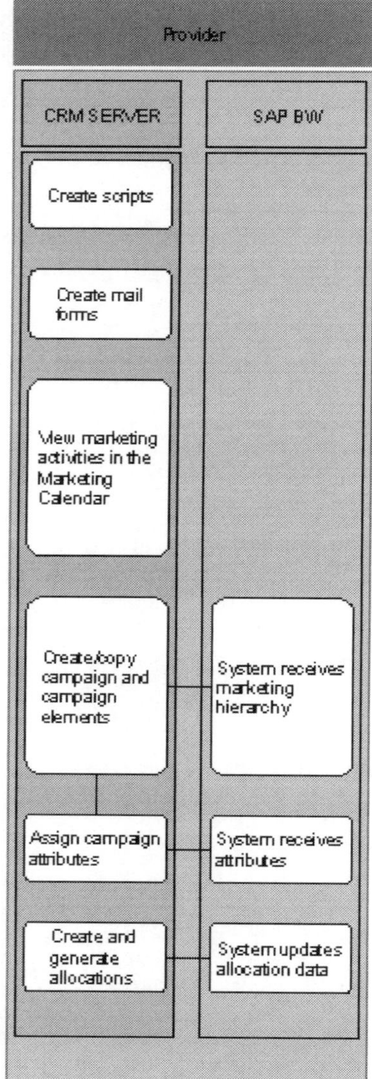
Provider
CRM SERVER
SAP BW
Create scripts
Create mail forms
View marketing activities in the Marketing Calendar
Create/copy campaign and campaign elements
System receives marketing hierarchy
Assign campaign attributes
System receives attributes
Create and generate allocations
System updates allocation data

Printed in Great Britain
by Amazon.co.uk, Ltd.,
Marston Gate.